Young people's influence and democratic education:
Ethnographic studies in upper secondary schools.

the Tufnell Press,
London,
United Kingdom

www.tufnellpress.co.uk

email contact@tufnellpress.co.uk

British Library Cataloguing-in-Publication Data
A catalogue record for this book is
available from the British Library

paperback	ISBN	1872767184
	ISBN-13	978-1-872767-18-5

Printed in England and U.S.A. by Lightning Source

Young people's influence and democratic education:
Ethnographic studies in upper secondary schools.

editors
Elisabet Öhrn
Lisbeth Lundahl
Dennis Beach

ETHNOGRAPHY AND EDUCATION

The *Ethnography and Education* book series aims to publish a range of authored and edited collections including both substantive research projects and methodological texts and in particular we hope to include recent PhDs. Our priority is for ethnographies that prioritise the experiences and perspectives of those involved and that also reflect a sociological perspective with international significance. We are particularly interested in those ethnographies that explicate and challenge the effects of educational policies and practices and interrogate and develop theories about educational structures, policies and experiences. We value ethnographic methodology that involves long-term engagement with those studied in order to understand their cultures, that use multiple methods of generating data and that recognise the centrality of the researcher in the research process.

www.ethnographyandeducation.org

The editors welcome substantive proposals that seek to:
> explicate and challenge the effects of educational policies and practices and
> interrogate and develop theories about educational structures, policies and
> experiences,
> highlight the agency of educational actors,
> provide accounts of how the everyday practices of those engaged in education are
> instrumental in social reproduction.

The editors are
> Professor Dennis Beach, University College of Borås, Sweden,
> Bob Jeffrey, (Commissioning Editor), The Open University,
> Professor Geoff Troman, Roehampton University, London and
> Professor Geoffrey Walford, University of Oxford.

Titles in the series include,

> Creative learning: European experiences, edited by Bob Jeffrey;

> Researching education policy: Ethnographic experiences, Geoff Troman, Bob Jeffrey and Dennis Beach;

> The commodification of teaching and learning, Dennis Beach and Marianne Dovemark;

> Performing English with a postcolonial accent: Ethnographic narratives from Mexico, Angeles Clemente and Michael J. Higgins.

> How to do Educational Ethnography edited by Geoffrey Walford

> Ritual and Identity; The staging and performing of rituals in the lives of young people, Christoph Wulf et al.

Contents

The authors

Dennis Beach is Professor of Education at the Universities of Borås and Gothenburg in Sweden. His main research area is in teacher education and the sociology of education, with a special interest in race and class.

Marianne Dovemark is an Associate Professor in education studies at the School of Education and Behavioural Sciences, University of Borås, Sweden and a senior lecturer in education at Gothenburg University. Her main research interests are in educational ethnography related to issues of social background, ethnicity and pupil influence in school.

Carina Hjelmér is a doctoral student in the Department of Applied Educational Science at Umeå University, Sweden. Her current research interests include democratic education and students' influence in schools, with special focus on gender and class perspectives.

Lisbet Lundahl is Professor at Department of Applied Educational Science, Umeå University. Her research mainly concerns education policy and politics, and young people's transitions from school to work in individual, institutional and political perspectives. Presently she runs two major research projects: 'Upper secondary school as a market' and 'Unsafe transitions, a longitudinal study of young people with incomplete upper secondary education'.

Elizabeth Öhrn is Professor of Education at the University of Gothenburg in Sweden. Her main research area is the sociology of education, with a special interest in power processes, gender, class and ethnicity..

Per-Åke Rosvall is a doctoral student at the School of Education and Behavioural Sciences, University of Borås, Sweden. His main research interests are in educational ethnography related to issues of social background, gender and pupil influence in school.

Chapter 1

Young people's influence and democratic education: Introduction

Dennis Beach and Elisabet Öhrn

This book is in large part about the ways that young people are able to act in school in order to raise discussions about and influence their schooling. It is based on a research project in the Swedish upper secondary school with the title *Active citizenship? On democratic education in the upper secondary school*, funded by The Swedish Research Council (VR 2006-2694). The project started in 2007 and is now drawing to an end. In this first chapter we present the background of the project and provide a brief outline of its focus, theoretical starting points and methods.

The research was prompted by our interest in democratic education and power relations (e.g. Beach, 1999b, 2003; Öhrn, 2001; Lahelma and Öhrn, 2003; Dovemark, 2004a, 2004b; Hansson and Lundahl, 2004; Arnesen and Lundahl, 2006), particularly in processes related to democracy in school which students themselves actively drive (e.g. Öhrn, 1998, 2009; Nyroos, Rönnberg and Lundahl, 2004). However, whereas contemporary research focusing on democracy in formal schooling is largely separated from analyses of young people's initiatives, the project set out to develop knowledge about the content and organisation of teaching and learning, as well as attempts by students to actively discuss and influence their schooling. The latter has sometimes been seen as an aspect of 'active citizenship' or 'living democracy' (OECD, 2005). In the project we were interested in investigating the rules and the social, cultural and material resources that young people apply when they behave as active, democratic citizens in the upper secondary school context.

Our research has been conducted with a special focus on gender in relation to social background as these relations appear to be highly relevant to processes of democracy and student influence in school. Accordingly, students from differently gendered and classed upper secondary programmes have been examined in the project. More detailed descriptions of the Swedish upper-secondary school, including its policy history and programme construction, are given in the next chapter.

Academic, vocational and individual programmes (see chapter two for definitions and discussion of these programmes) have been analysed in the project, using ethnographic approaches, including participant observation, discussions and formal interviews with five groups of students.

The principle research questions addressed in the project were:

1. What values and understandings of citizenship and democracy are expressed in the researched education processes?
2. How is the education organised with respect to influence from the students? What possibilities do they have to discuss issues related to democracy, to challenge the teaching content and to articulate criticism?
3. Do students act in relation to democracy issues and conditions in the classroom and the wider school context and, if so, in which contexts? How does the school relate to this?

Questions such as these are primarily concerned with young peoples' experiences of, attitudes to, and practices of democracy in formal education spaces. We hold that they are particularly important in the present era, not least because young people are spending increasing amounts of time in formal education. Almost all young people in Sweden today continue to study after compulsory school in upper secondary school, and universities have become more common post-school options than conventional workplaces for young adults; about forty-five per cent of a cohort begin higher education by the age of twenty-five (Eriksson, 2009). Thus, the experience of democratic participation among the young (including young voters) is strongly related to education spaces. This underlines the importance of the ways in which democratic issues are treated and respected in schools and other educational settings.

Previous research of relevance to the project

Research on democratic education versus youth and power
The project is related to two research fields: one focuses on democratic education and the other on the positions of power available to young adults and how they mount initiatives that affect schools. Swedish policy texts hold both as highly important. The Swedish national curriculum for upper secondary schools emphasises that the schools should both communicate democratic values to their students and teach in democratic ways that create possibilities for student influence (Ministry of Education and Research, 1994; see also chapter two).

Empirical research projects to date have tended to focus on one or the other of these aspects rather than their interrelations.

With respect to the teaching of democratic values, international research has shown that some change has occurred in school practices in recent years. The very meaning of democracy is said to be changing and to refer, increasingly, to 'unregulated business manoeuvres in a free-market economy' (Apple and Beane, 2007, p. 150). Education policy analysis has suggested that this is due to an input from a contemporary neo-liberal approach to education that emphasises individual freedom of choice and individual rights, at the expense of collective justice and equality, with a shift in focus from democracy in society to individual choice (Englund, 2003; Gordon, Lahelma and Beach, 2003; Beach 2008c, 2010). The main issues stressed in teaching are the individual's rights as an autonomous actor in relation to the State and the communication of factual knowledge; much less attention is paid to political criticism and reflection.

This pattern can also be observed at the Swedish upper-secondary level in the use of individual teaching materials that emphasise factual knowledge of formal democracy and formal democratic influence (Bronäs, 2003). Collective action (e.g. demonstrations and other forms of public protest available to sections of the population that lack voting rights) that youth has typically engaged in, has been marginalised in teaching.

Research on student influence shows from its perspective that the possibilities young people have for making a difference in school today are limited, and tend to concern the basic organisation of day-to-day learning plans (Dovemark, 2004a). Issues related to more fundamental, collective issues, such as the unequal distribution of rights in society and the situations of subordinate groups and struggles against oppressive practices, both in and outside schools as institutions, such as racist acts, are less common (Öhrn, 1998).

Classroom discussions on such issues might help to contest teacher positions, as they raise a variety of opinions, and those held by the teacher are not necessarily accepted by the students (Liljestrand, 2002). Some studies (e.g. Davies, 2002) suggest that Swedish classrooms are relatively open and more readily promote deliberative conversations than counterparts in many other countries. However, as noted by Arnot and Reay (2007, p. 322), having one's say in class by no means implies influence; it may simply obscure power relations and school stratification.

Research from Scandinavia and other parts of the world call attention to gender and class relations as central issues in all aspects of democratic education.

This is manifested, for instance, in often voiced concerns about the democratic vision and conduct of young people, particularly young men from low-income, marginalised and territorially stigmatised areas (Bunar, 2008). Both the Swedish media and politicians have recurrently drawn attention to violence and racist acts by these groups and in these areas, and there has been an upsurge of anti-immigration sentiment in society. As problems of racism and violence become more severe, there are increasingly urgent demands for schools to take measures by tending more specifically to the education of these boys (see Öhrn, 2001).

Research on gendered and classed school practices

The report of the Swedish Democracy Survey (Demokratiutredningen, 2000) describes a lack of democratic schooling and signs of reduced involvement in political parties and electoral participation amongst young people. It also refers to investigations showing that youngsters today experience a large measure of powerlessness in relation to politics, despite having significant interest in political issues. These issues have also been examined through questionnaire surveys to upper-secondary students and they report of considerable variations in the knowledge about democracy held by these young adults (Swedish National Agency for Education, 2003). For instance, the young men surveyed showed more competence in addressing questions relating to the economy, whilst young women addressed questions about equality and human rights better than young men.

Differences between students from different kinds of upper-secondary school study programme were also noted. One point of particular interest was that knowledge about formal democracy was most limited in students taking the male-dominated vocational programmes. Another was that young men commonly discuss politics with their peers, whilst young women do so with their teachers. This indicates that the schools' discussion of these issues may include girls to a greater extent than boys.

Occasional studies suggest that girls in Swedish secondary schools have developed greater social and moral understanding than boys (Svingby, 1993) and, hence, there is a great need to develop the teaching of boys in these respects (Swedish National Agency for Education, 1999). However, no research supports the idea that schooling promotes girls' development of democratic values more than that of boys, or indeed that boys in general should act in less democratic ways. If anything, contemporary research rather suggests that issues such as these have a weak position in general (Dovemark, 2004a). They are not given much attention in teaching, and they tend to become gendered through marginalisation effects; social and democratic issues are separated from the common, general education as private projects for girls and at best peripheral projects for boys (Öhrn, 1998, 2001). This does not provide the girls with an influential position to act on such democratic issues, rather it reflects the traditional expectations of female responsibility in school (cf. Walkerdine, 1990).

Furthermore, studies of young people's attempts to influence the educational context do not lend support to notions that school environments generally favour girls' understanding and behaviour more than those of boys. Instead, most research related to these issues suggests that they are more orientated towards groups of boys and certain masculinities. For instance, course content is said to relate more to traditionally male than to female practices (Paechter 1998), citizenship to be constructed more often as masculine, and Eurocentric, than as feminine (Gordon and Holland, 2003) and groups of boys are described as influencing teaching more than girls through their dominance of public speech and space (e.g. Wilson, 1991; Lynch and Lodge, 2002; Lahelma and Öhrn, 2003).

There are some exceptions to the above points. For instance, some investigations indicate that middle-class girls can act as individualised learners by managing to construct dialogues with teachers, and thus communicate their opinions and concerns, better than other groups (e.g. Arnot, 2006). In addition, some studies of processes in comprehensive schools have indicated that girls try to influence classroom practices via collective actions more than boys, and thus are more able to act as motors of change (Öhrn, 2004).

These results could be seen as conflicting with the assertions about boys' prominent position in school. However, they might also be interpreted as meaning that boys—given their position as a group in class—have less reason to take action to adapt school routines and content to their own interests as these interests are already those that are mainly represented. Another interpretation is that active change requires positive school engagement, which seems to be more unusual amongst boys as a whole than amongst girls, and deemed to be more compatible with accepted femininities than masculinities (cf. Epstein, 1998). Similarly, Davies (2002, p. 47) suggests that arenas of formal student influence, e.g. class and school councils, might be associated with caring, and may thus be stereotypically related to female involvement in contrast to the public image traditionally associated with wider politics. Research showing that both genders initiate, take a lead in, and participate in acts of public collective resistance against targets outside school in local politics appears to support this interpretation (Öhrn, 2004, 2005).

Research on masculinities, femininities and sub-cultural formations

Previous research indicates that school involvement of various kinds is at odds with dominant youth masculinities, particularly those associated with migrant sub-cultures and the working class (Frosh, Phoenix and Pattman, 2002; Archer and Francis, 2005), and that boys tend to distance themselves from the school's theoretical orientation and develop alternative masculinities to those valued by the formal institution (e.g. Kryger, 1990; Smith, 2007). This understanding is not new, but it has new connotations in the present age, associated with issues related to de-industrialisation in Western societies. Due to de-industrialisation, extended contact with educational institutions has become a new norm for young men who in previous eras would have made an early transition from school to work as an alternative to unemployment. This is assumed to have affected constructions of masculinity; as paid manual labour disappears, so too do the foundations of conventional working class masculinities as a basis for social influence (Weis, 1990). For the same reason, collective action based on a male sub-culture connected to labouring, as often occurred in the 1970s (Willis, 1977), is now less likely (Öhrn, 2002b; Willis, 2004).

Through their historical relationship to schooling girls can be imagined as having been able to develop better collective understanding of how to deal with relative subordination of the kinds embedded in de-industrialisation than young men have. Girls with a working-class background in Sweden have often needed educational qualifications to find work and seem partly to have adjusted to this. However, there are also other developments that may have assisted them. Parallel to the changes in labour processes in western society there have been changes brought about through social movements such as feminism, which have provided young women with more powerful platforms than previously available to them from which to develop their views and actions (Arnot, David and Weiner, 1999). Berggren (2001) shows, for example, how the secondary school transition of working-class girls is characterised by the development of networks that give them some space to act in school. Such networks appear to be essential in classroom practice in order for the girls to establish positions of influence (Gordon, Holland and Lahelma, 2000), pursue political interests (Öhrn, 1998) and challenge any actions that may deny them their full rights (Skeggs, 1991).

Research has provided few examples of boys establishing these kinds of networks. Theoretical explanations for this lack have already been mentioned, but it should also be noted that boys and masculinities have been less heavily researched than girls and femininities in Scandinavian contexts. Scandinavian research on these issues differs from other, for instance British, research where boys and masculinities have been the focus for decades (see Öhrn and Weiner, 2009). However, the larger body of research on males/masculinities in Britain has not focused on their networking and attempts to exert influence in school, hence there is a lack of knowledge about the collective influence of boys and their relationships in school (Öhrn, 2002a). Indeed, there is not much knowledge about any collective actions to influence education. As noted by Hatcher (2002, p. 63 in Davies 2004, p. 54) there has been a general lack of discussion of collective resistance in the academic debate on education in Britain, and the same could be said about Sweden and the other Scandinavian countries.

Project theory, methods and analysis

Theory
Gender emerges in the discussion above as a major division in relation to schooling about democracy, but in conflicting ways. Understandings of various aspects of citizenship appear to be constructed largely as masculine in school, and both old and recent studies indicate that the school is an arena where traditionally male activities and male players dominate. However, some overviews of democratic aspects of schooling indicate that boys perform at a lower standard on democracy-related issues than girls, and are less likely to be engaged in democracy-related activities and issues in school.

The two research fields discussed earlier—i.e. research on teaching and research on students' actions in relation to democracy—are quite distinctly two separate fields. Consequently, we have limited knowledge about how student influence relates to the teaching of democracy, and a major aim of the project this book is based upon was to address this lack of knowledge. Moreover, given the indications that processes and practices in education are gendered, classed and raced, the empirical parts of the project were largely developed from pertinent gender theory and feminist perspectives on citizenship and democratic education (Yuval-Davis, 1997; Arnot and Dillabough, 2000; Gordon and Holland, 2003; Arnot, 2006; Gordon, 2006). In addition we initially took on board Giddens' theory of structuration (1984) in our analyses of the rules and resources that are used by (or are potentially available to) students wishing to influence schools and schooling. These served as general theoretical starting points for the project and provided initial foci for the data production. However, as will be discussed below, we also took an ethnographic approach. This involved the production and analysis of materials developed from multiple sources and perspectives, and led us to experiment with and find value in other theoretical perspectives (see also Willis, 2000; Willis and Trondman, 2000; Trondman, 2008).

Methods

Previous research indicates that urban working class and migrant sub-cultural masculinities particularly tend to oppose academic learning (e.g. Epstein, 1998; Phoenix, 2004). For the project, this underscored the need to include different contexts, particularly those that are less academically and more 'vocationally' or 'practically' oriented in the research. Theoretically, one could postulate that environments with clear links to influential forms of traditional male working-class organisation, such as trade-unionism, party-political affiliation, or local health and work-safety activities could provide more favourable conditions than traditional academic classroom activities for working class boys to exert influence. As mentioned above, the ability of these boys to establish a strong counterculture in today's extended academic schooling is questioned (Weis, 1990; Öhrn, 2002b). However, this does not mean that traditionally male-profession-oriented courses (such as construction or car-maintenance) cannot provide forms for facilitating such organisation.

In the research we have included both vocational and academic programmes, centred in both traditionally male and traditionally female domains: the Natural Sciences and Social Sciences Programmes from the academic domain and the Vehicle and Child and Recreation Programmes from the vocational domain. We also investigated the Individual Programme. These programmes are described in more detail in the next chapter.

Analysis

When analysing the impact young people may have on school practice an initial focus was, in line with Giddens (1984), on the rules and resources used in schools when teaching about democracy-related issues or encouraging students to engage in democratic action. In Giddens' work resources refer to capacities to influence the physical and social environment. These resources can be provided in school practice, but they may also emanate from, for example, the political experiences or social networks of young people outside the school. The concept of rules refers to spoken and unspoken expectations of behaviour in social life, and hence what one might expect from one's social environment. In this manner, rules provide tools to orient interpretations and actions.

We have examined forms of teaching in Swedish upper secondary school, in relation to the issues described above, in terms of two fundamental dimensions: (i.) ways in which the formal organisation of the education encourages (or hinders) young people to express criticism and develop strategies to influence their schooling, and (ii.) informal processes that encourage or hinder relevant conduct.

Previous investigations suggest that teaching forms that aim to activate student influence, such as the use of deliberative conversation, create spaces for various arguments and elements of 'collective will-formation' (Englund, 2000, p. 6), as does regular political education in which teachers and students develop strategies for change (Öhrn, 2005). However, of particular interest in the analysis of teaching in our research is Gordon's (2006) distinction between education for *future or present citizenship*, that is whether pupils 'are encouraged to act 'like' citizens whilst their duties are emphasised more than their rights, or whether they are allowed and encouraged to 'act' citizenship in everyday life in the present' (p. 3). Gordon emphasises the particular importance of being active, i.e. of students being 'agentic individual citizens' (2006, p. 1).

Gordon also highlights the problem of the focus on individual aspects of citizenship in schools, i.e. the concentration on autonomy and individualism rather than collective action. In the project we have been particularly interested in whether different groups of young people themselves are challenging such an understanding, and the objectives and forms of change that they may formulate. This has been investigated in previous studies of both public education and informal peer groups. The latter are essential for analysing the development and positioning of various kinds of masculinity and femininity within an institution (Connell, 1987; Connell and Messerschmidt, 2005). Therefore, in the project fieldwork we have paid attention to processes both during lessons and in other parts of the school day, focusing on both targets for change and processes of negotiation.

Complementary theoretical perspectives
As mentioned above, feminist perspectives (especially on citizenship), and Giddens' theory of structuration, served as general theoretical starting points for the project and provided initial foci for the data production. However,

in accordance with the methodological approach chosen, a need for other theoretical perspectives was identified during the fieldwork and analyses. Bernstein's theory of pedagogical transmission from his work concerning pedagogical modalities and communication, was one of these. In particular we have used his concepts of classification and framing, and visible and invisible pedagogy. The classification and framing concepts we applied were those formulated initially in Bernstein (1971, 1975 and 1990), in which the following sets of principles are said to regulate most communicative contexts in education (see also Beach, 1995):

1. Interactional principles, which regulate the selection, organisation, sequencing, and pacing of communication.
2. Locational principles, which regulate the physical location and form of realisation (i.e. the range of objects, their attributes, their relation to each other and the space in which they are constituted)

The relationships between these two sets of principles constitute the *classification* and *framing* of pedagogical discourse and instruction insofar that the stronger the tie between the interactional (temporal) and locational (spatial) features of the communicative context, the stronger will be its classification, and the stronger the classification the more likely that the array of objects, attributes represented and their relations within the communicative context will have a fixed relation to each other and will be highly specific to that context. In this sense the term classification refers to the level of specialisation in terms of the degree of insulation between categories of discourse, agents, practices and contexts and provides rules for both transmitters and acquirers for the recognition of the degree of specialisation of their texts and their contextual (pedagogic/educational) legitimacy. Academic disciplines like physics are said to provide examples of highly specialised discourses and (thus) highly classified educational content according to Bernstein (1990, p. 34).

Using Bernstein's concepts

The concept of classification is often used together with the concept of framing. However, framing refers to the order and regulation of control over the selection of sequencing, pacing, and criterial rules of the pedagogic act and describes therefore firstly the communicative relationship between transmitters and acquirers of pedagogical discourses and secondly the knowledge mediated by these discourses (Bernstein, 1990, p. 214). Where the educator's control over framing relations is weak, the acquirer has greater influence over the regulation of the communicative features that help constitute the communicative context and its legitimate discourses. Where it is strong they do not. Different combinations of classification and framing form different pedagogical codes and constitute different pedagogic forms. Bernstein (1975) developed the terms visible and invisible pedagogy to refer to these different modalities (Bernstein, 1990, p. 53) and are presented in the table below.

The visible pedagogic model	The invisible pedagogic model
1. Comprises a context of reproduction developed around groups which are homogenous in terms of ability. It uses privatised and competitive (individuated) acts of knowledge acquisition and assessment.	1. Is less concerned to produce explicit stratifying differences between learners as it is less interested in external and more interested in internal standards.
2. Involves a progression guided by the logical order of presentation in discipline content, structure and relations.	2. Does not focus on external, gradable performances by the learner. The intention is rather more to shape contexts and environments to enable externalisation-internalisation processes of individual knowledge construction and sharing between people involved in teaching and learning activities in group contexts.
3. Has a pedagogic medium that is characterised by a social relation of superiority from teacher down to learner.	
4. Encourages a learning situation with strong pacing following strict sequencing rules in two sites of learning: the lecture and the home/free-time situation. Text-books and lecture note taking make this possible, instruction pace makes it imperative. The relation between learning in the two sites is regulated by strong framing characteristics in the first.	3. Is contrite to emphasise the development of competence rather than the learning of facts.
	4. Creates spaces in discourse and activities to be filled by learners.
5. Communication between transmitters and receivers of knowledge is constituted by strong classification and framing, even under conditions of surface opposition. Time is treated as scarce and this strictly regulates the rules which restrict what are constituted and regarded as legitimate written and spoken texts, question and answer format, their contexts, their social relations of production and discourse boundaries.	5. Because of its nature, hiding the rules of hierarchy and order which operate within institutions like schools, the model is problematic in practice because many highly motivated learners will always look for the standards by which they are measured and will have difficulties in understanding what is expected of them when they cannot locate these in clear, decisive and concrete forms.
	6. The model does not match what learners expect and are used to because it does not fit the way education is usually organised in schools in societies like ours.
6. There is an emphasis on an economy of transmission, as the students are compacted into mass populated small areas for instruction purposes, and because as much (or more) time is spent learning outside of schedule time as in it.	7. There are thus contradictions created by the distributive rules of the model, such that its (intended) pedagogy does not reproduce desired pedagogic discourses in practice. What is acquired is not usually what is intended.

The organisation of the book

This first chapter briefly presents the research background and the conceptual backdrop to the empirical study. A further contextualisation of the study is given in chapter two, in which Swedish upper secondary school and its policy history are presented, together with some details about the study programmes it offers. The chapter discusses developments in organisation and policies over the last four decades; and also describes the class, gender and ethnicity characteristics of the cohorts enrolled on the programmes. The book's third chapter introduces the methodology and provides comprehensive descriptions of the design, implementation and analysis procedures.

The next five chapters are empirical. Each is based on fieldwork related to a particular programme and focuses on the book's main questions about young people's democratic education and participation. However, each chapter has a slightly different focus, depending on aspects found to be central through the field work: chapters four and five are most focused on young people's actions to affect their school, while chapters six, seven and eight focus more on the conditions of influence in terms of pedagogical framing, form and content. In chapter nine we attempt to synthesise results from the empirical work, as described in the preceding chapters, under themes relating to central aspects of democratic education and student influence.

Chapter 2

Swedish upper secondary education: Policy and organisational context

Lisbeth Lundahl

Introduction

The Swedish upper secondary school, *gymnasieskolan*, as organised from the early 1990s to 2011 (when a major reform comes into force), constitutes the context of the book and the present chapter provides a brief background to the ethnographic studies that comprise its empirical component. It is divided into three sections. The first section briefly describes *reforms and changes to the governance* of upper secondary education during the last four decades. The second section highlights the *curriculum*, describing major characteristics and some aspects of the academic, vocational and individual programs. Education for democracy and citizenship in upper secondary education and the space and arguments for student influence are discussed. The third section concerns *the students* in the upper secondary school; their study choices and their paths through and after upper secondary education related to their class, gender and ethnic background.

In several important respects *gymnasieskolan* is a coherent and inclusive educational institution. It builds on nine years of comprehensive, compulsory and extensive (in international terms) public primary and pre-schooling and embraces almost all 16-19 year-olds, with seemingly equivalent academic and vocational programmes. With one exception all progammes are three-years in duration, they have a common national curriculum plan and core subjects, and provide general eligibility to higher education.

Gymnasieskolan

Swedish education, from pre-school to university level, rests on ideas that free education of high and equal standard should be available to all children and young people, regardless of their origin, and together with those in Denmark, Finland and Norway, Swedish upper secondary level schools are among the least socially segregated in the world (Jenkins, Micklewright and Schnepf, 2006). Nevertheless, flaws in this idealised vision of *Gymnasieskolan* are readily apparent, including: growing local and regional differences between schools and between vocational and academic programmes; divisions and inequalities related to gender, social class and ethnicity; tensions and dilemmas arising from local fragmentation and the market situation in which today's upper secondary schools have to work. Furthermore, the marked division between the academic and vocational paths re-introduced by the 2009 upper secondary school reform represents a clear break with previous efforts towards integration.

Reforms and governance changes

The reforms of Swedish secondary education during the last fifty years have consistently had economic as well as social purposes, although the balance between social and economic objectives has changed over time (Lundahl, 1997, 1998, 2002; Lundahl et al., 2010). The reforms have largely aimed to weaken the strong division between academic and vocational tracks, and thus satisfy demands to provide more flexible and skilled manpower, promote equality and social justice, foster responsible and active citizens, and avoid educational blind-alleys that could lead to unemployment and insecurity. The promotion of individual needs and demands has become an increasingly important aim, but the economic and social-reproductive functions of education are still major concerns.

The first cycle of comprehensive reforms (the 1960s)

The present upper-secondary school builds on a number of older schools and traditions. Through a reform in 1964, academic secondary schools (*läroverk*), technical schools and schools of commerce were gathered into a unified organisation, and a few years later, in 1968, two-year post-compulsory vocational education, shorter vocational courses and two-year continuation schools were added to the programmes offered by the comprehensive upper-secondary school, which were hereafter attended by most 15-19 year-olds. The reform was the first step in a process of successively bringing vocational and academic programmes closer to each other. An important aim was to place theoretical and practical education on a more equal footing, but the reform was also an attempt to meet rising educational demands and address a perceived mismatch between the existing curricula and the needs of working life. As in subsequent reforms, curriculum broadening and flexibility were advocated (Govt. Bill 1968:140, p. 11).

Experiments and investigations (the 1970s and 1980s)
The upper-secondary school reforms of the 1960s were drafted and implemented during a time of optimism about the future, steady economic growth and prolonged social democratic rule, but these trends were broken in the 1970s, when political and economic circumstances became much more unstable and uncertain. Partly due to pressure from the major national unions, a public committee was appointed by the social democratic Minister of Education in 1976 to assess ways to improve and develop upper secondary education. However, the committee's directives were soon modified by the new conservative-liberal-centre coalition government, the first government in Sweden that was not led by the Social Democratic Party (*Socialdemokratiska Arbetarepartiet, SAP*) since the early 1930s. Nearly a decade of local experiments followed, largely addressing instructional methods and the inner work of schools, but eventually also the modernisation of vocational education and training (Bergström, 1993; Lundahl, 1997).

The second cycle of comprehensive reform (the 1990s)
In 1991 an upper secondary school reform, initiated by a social democratic government, was launched, and a new national curriculum plan and syllabi for post-compulsory education was introduced in 1994 (Ministry of Education and Research, 1994). The 1991 reform, to be fully implemented in 1995/96, was based on arguments similar to those of the late 1970s: current upper secondary education was too inflexible and risked creating deadlocks; the needs of students, parents and other local actors were insufficiently acknowledged; vocational education did not provide the basic knowledge required in modern working life; and more generally changes to upper secondary education were needed to meet the requirements of rapidly changing working life.

The new upper school reform added a third year to the vocational education programme, and a programme to be tailored to individual needs. A common core of subjects was established for all national and specially designed programmes, which were supposed to provide general eligibility for higher education. Of the sixteen original national programmes (in 1998 yet another, the technology programme, was created) fourteen included vocational preparation. Although the national and special programmes shared certain characteristics, the special programmes could be adapted, for instance to local and regional needs. The individual programme was intended to meet needs of students with uncertain study plans. It could be of varying length and content, and incorporate (for instance) apprenticeship training. Young people's right to upper secondary education was now enshrined by law, and the municipalities were obliged to offer a broad variety of national programmes, primarily related to the interests of the students (Govt. Bill 1990/91:85). In other words, the kinds of upper secondary education offered by each municipality were to be no longer primarily dictated by anticipated labour market needs, decided at national and regional levels, as was the case before the 1990s.

The extension of the vocational programmes and the integration of educational contents at the heart of the 1991 reform was far from uncontroversial. According to the conservative and liberal parties, the preparation for higher education would be undermined, and it was a waste of resources to force young people to study longer than necessary. However, while in office in 1991-94 they made no efforts to change the reforms. In contrast, one of the first measures of the conservative-liberal coalition government in office from the fall of 2006 was to initiate a reform intended to divide upper secondary education into three distinctly different streams—education preparing for further studies, vocational education and apprenticeship training—only one of which was to provide direct access to higher education. As mentioned above, a change in this direction will be introduced in 2011.

Extensive local autonomy and semi-market conditions (1990s and early 2000s)
As in most other OECD countries, the public sector in Sweden generally, and education in particular, was transformed in the 1980s and 1990s by changes including deregulation, decentralisation and marketisation, driven by desires to introduce or enhance freedom of choice, entrepreneurialism, competition and new modes of public management. These reforms are normally understood to be a project developed by the political right-wing. However, in Sweden they were initiated by both social democratic and conservative-liberal coalition governments in the late 1980s and early 1990s, albeit with partly differing motives. They have strongly affected the Swedish upper secondary school system, which has become of the most decentralised educational systems in Europe since the beginning of the 1990s.

Roughly speaking, the State formulates educational objectives in the form of national curriculum plans and syllabi, and evaluates the quality and outcomes of education, while local authorities and schools enjoy considerable autonomy in allocating resources and time, class sizes, selection of educational methods, textbooks, and so on. This is in sharp contrast to the situation in the preceding forty-year period. This period was characterised by strong state governance, in particular through detailed economic steering. So consequently, the local variations, both between and within municipalities, have increased vastly since then, and it is no exaggeration to characterise the current situation as highly fragmented. The changes to the division of responsibilities introduced in the early 1990s have also (*inter alia*) given the so-called school professionals—principals and teachers—far greater responsibility and freedom.

A veritable upper secondary school market, underpinned by ideas of freedom of choice and promotion of quality in schools through competition, has developed and become increasingly influential; in the early 2000s competition and other expressions of the educational market were manifested in almost all upper secondary schools (Swedish National Agency for Education, 2010c). The introduction in 1992 of generous subsidies for 'independent schools' ('free-schools' in everyday discourse), tax-funded schools run by various bodies, such as private companies, religious and other organisations—led to a rapid growth of such schools, particularly at upper secondary level and in urban areas. In 2009/10, more than a fifth of all upper secondary students attended an independent school, but with large local variations; in some big city areas the independent schools attracted up to half of all students.

Originally consisting of single smaller schools, the free-school sector has been rapidly transformed into a capitalist business like any other in the 2000s, featuring big school corporation chains, PLCs, and profit-making. Furthermore, in contrast to the situation in almost all other countries, the owners are allowed to pocket profits (Erixon Arreman and Holm, 2011). However, there is also substantial competition between public upper secondary schools, because from 2008 students have been able to choose schools freely, without being tied to their own municipality. Hence, especially in urban regions, they encounter a huge, motley smorgasbord of courses and programmes, resulting both from the marketisation and the 1991 reforms, which gave considerable freedom to create local programmes and specialisations.

Today, most upper secondary schools invest large resources in marketing their education, using various channels, such as fairs, web-pages, written material and advertisements in newspapers, TV and radio. In addition, principals, career counsellors, teachers and students are engaged in marketing their schools (Erixon

Arreman, Lundahl and Schedin, 2009; Swedish National Agency for Education, 2010c; Erixon Arreman and Holm, 2011).

Preparing for higher studies, working life and participation in society

A common structure

At the time of writing, upper secondary schools offer (and will offer until 2011) prospective students 17 three-year *national programmes, specially designed* programmes, and the *Individual programme*—the length of which varies between individuals (Figure 2.1).

Figure 2.1 Upper Secondary School programme structure

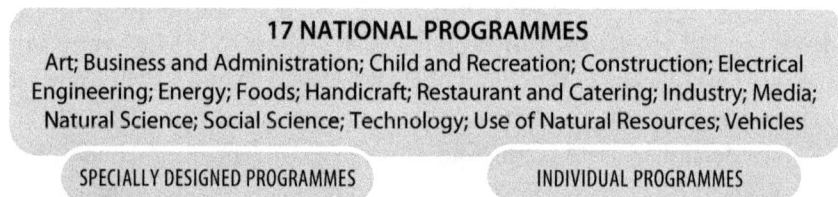

17 NATIONAL PROGRAMMES
Art; Business and Administration; Child and Recreation; Construction; Electrical Engineering; Energy; Foods; Handicraft; Restaurant and Catering; Industry; Media; Natural Science; Social Science; Technology; Use of Natural Resources; Vehicles

SPECIALLY DESIGNED PROGRAMMES   INDIVIDUAL PROGRAMMES

All three-year programmes provide eligibility for higher education, although three of the national programmes (natural science, social science and technology) are commonly described as mainly preparing for further studies, while the remaining fourteen are predominantly regarded as being oriented towards vocational preparation. But this is not a formal or official distinction, and some of the so-called vocational programmes have only weak connections to the labour market. The three-year programmes comprise eight core subjects with common syllabi and goals: Swedish (or Swedish as a second language), English, social studies, religion, mathematics, science, physical education and health, and arts. Approximately a third of the time is allotted to the core subjects. The remaining time is devoted to different subjects, in line with the profile of the national programme, and individual options. All national programmes except the Health Programme include national or local specialisations of varying degrees. More generally, the vocational programmes preparing for male-dominated occupations have a higher degree of specialisation than those preparing for female-dominated occupations (cf. Arnman and Järnek, 2006). The specially designed programmes offer more flexibility than the national programmes, and are frequently highlighted in the profiling and marketing of schools mentioned above. Within the three year programmes, students select fields of study and may choose individual courses, in some cases accounting for up to a third of the total time, i.e. student choices are not limited to school and programme (cf. Lund, 2008). In order to be accepted for a national or specially designed programme, a student has to obtain at least passes in Swedish, English and mathematics, or is otherwise referred to an individual programme.

As mentioned above, since the 1990s the municipalities have had the freedom and responsibility to decide which programmes to offer, and as far as possible to meet the demands of the students. However, some young people are not awarded their first choices; in 2008/09 on average eighty-one per cent of all applicants for the national programmes got their first choice, and somewhat lower proportions of male students and students with non-Swedish origins, with considerable variations between the programmes (see also table 2.1). These figures and those in the following sections are based on statistics from the Swedish National Agency for Education (2010d) and refer to the 2008-2009 academic year, unless otherwise indicated.

Since the late 1960s there are no final examinations in either the Swedish nine-year compulsory school or upper secondary school. Instead, final certificates based on marks obtained in each subject (compulsory school) and courses within subjects (upper secondary school) are awarded. The fact that every course—small or large, early or late in the studies—is marked and counts towards the final certificate of upper secondary education has been criticised for causing stress among both students and teachers (Ministry of Education and Research, 2008). Certain changes in these respects, e.g. the introduction of an upper secondary diploma, will take place from 2011.

Vocational programmes
Two of the most controversial aspects of the 1991 reform concerned the prolongation of the vocational programmes with a third year and the increased proportions of 'general' or 'academic' subjects. However, another aspect (which is not often mentioned), is that the reform also increased the time allotted to vocationally-oriented subject content. As in the situation before the 1990s, most of the vocational education and training is school-based, but all vocational programmes are supposed to include at least fifteen weeks of education located at places of work (*arbetsplatsförlagd utbildning, APU*). In many cases, however, this requirement is only partly met, or not met at all, often because of a lack of time and/or other resources at workplaces (Ministry of Education and Research, 2008) and according to an evaluation in 1998, up to forty per cent of

the vocational students did not receive a fifteen week APU. The situation was re-evaluated in 2010, but the results are not yet available.

The high percentage of vocational teachers lacking teacher qualifications is another considerable problem and will be exacerbated by extensive shortages of such teachers when most of them retire in the near future. The division between 'vocational' and 'academic' can be clearly seen in the educational and other requirements of different teacher categories at upper secondary level. The current education of vocational teachers is the shortest of all teacher categories—formally three years, but often much shorter in reality. Following a new teacher education reform, coming into force in 2012, the duration of the initial training will be halved to eighteen months for vocational teachers, but certainly not for teachers of the academic subjects.

In many teachers' opinions, the goals of the core subjects are set too high in relation to the ambitions and knowledge of the students and it is not unusual to ignore 'difficult' elements of the contents or reduce the requirements, so inevitably the students obtain low grades. In addition, many students perceive the instruction in core subjects as abstract, and they cannot see its use in their future work (Swedish National Agency for Education, 2000). In particular, mathematics is a stumbling-block for many students, but many also fail in sports and health, science, religion, social studies and Swedish B (the second course in Swedish at upper-secondary school), albeit with considerable variations between the vocational programmes (Ministry of Education and Research, 2008). However, the reduction in the time allotted for core subjects in vocational programmes of the future upper secondary school has been one of the most intensely debated and criticised aspects of the 2009 reform. Some critics fear that young people will be caught in deadlocks or will have difficulties completing their studies if they want to continue to higher education, but it is also argued that many of today's so-called manual jobs require (*inter alia*) much greater communication and language skills than previously (cf. Lindberg, 2003). The reform will give students on the vocational programmes a right to extended studies (worth 300 points, equivalent to twelve weeks of study) to be eligible for higher education, but critics argue that this will be insufficient.

Academic programmes

As noted above, the *gymnasieskolan* programmes are not formally defined as vocational or academic, but traditionally the Natural Science and Social Science programmes are regarded as the ones that prepare students for further studies.

Their curricular goals do not mention any vocational preparation, and both of these programmes, and the Technology and Arts programmes are excluded from the requirement for fifteen weeks of education at places of work. The curricular goals of the Natural Science Programme are more focused than those of the Social Science Programme, which is sometimes perceived as having too little profile by the students (Ministry of Education and Research, 2008).

Many of the specially designed programmes come close to the Social Science Programme, which may indicate a need for clearer orientation. Furthermore, complaints from tertiary level teachers that students acquire too little knowledge from upper secondary education (e.g. in Swedish, foreign languages, mathematics and science) have influenced the decisions to increase the distinctions between the programmes and increase the time allotted to certain academic subjects in programmes preparing students for higher studies in the recent upper secondary school reform (ibid.).

In contrast to the teachers of vocational subjects, teachers of all subjects on the academic programmes are supposed to have a long initial teacher education—five to five and a half years—and the coming reform of teacher education will increase requirements for deep subject knowledge and further specialisation.

The Individual Programme

The Individual Programme should generally be tailored to meet the needs of students who are not eligible or prepared to attend one of the three year programmes, but students may also follow an individual programme for other reasons (see below). Since 1998, when stricter rules of eligibility were introduced, the proportion of students attending the Individual Programme has been relatively stable, averaging seven to nine per cent, but with large local variations (see below). Students who lack passes in Swedish or Swedish as a second language, mathematics and English are not qualified for a national programme.

The Individual Programme has no common programme objectives or courses, and there is substantial local freedom to design the studies. For example, this programme may be organised and based separately from the other upper secondary education programmes. It may include courses from the national programmes, in so-called programme-oriented individual programmes (PRIV), but not necessarily. Young people who have newly arrived from another country and lack knowledge of Swedish are often placed in introductory classes within the Individual Programme (IVIK). The Individual Programme may also include vocational practice and apprenticeship training. However, the latter has attracted little interest in its present form from either young people or employers—in 2007 thirty students in total attended apprenticeship training at upper secondary level. However, apprenticeship training is meant to become a more common choice in the future, and a trial designed to develop such training has been undertaken in 2009-2010 (Lundahl et al., 2010).

Most of the students attend one year of studies at the Individual Programme, and around twenty per cent continue to a second or third year. The scope, organisation and contents of the Individual Programme display remarkable local variations. For example, the proportion of students attending this programme varied amongst municipalities from one to twenty-one per cent at the time of the study (2008/09). In addition, several evaluations have shown that the quality of the programme shows unacceptably large variations between different municipalities.

Certain efforts have been made at state level to improve this situation. Since 2006 municipalities have been obliged to offer full-time Individual Programmes, and a handbook for schools and municipalities on the quality and development of this programme has been issued (The Swedish National Agency for School Improvement, 2007). Nevertheless, recent reports indicate that local interpretations of what constitutes a 'sufficiently good' Individual Programmes still vary considerably, between and even within municipalities (Olofsson, Panican, Pettersson and Righard, 2010). With respect to the goal that students on the Individual Programme should become prepared to successfully attend a national or special programme, the outcomes are not very encouraging. In 2005, less than half of the students on the Individual Programme continued to a national programme, and only one in five completed upper secondary education within four years (Swedish National Agency for Education, 2007).

Student influence and democracy education
International-comparative studies show that democracy education is broadly defined in Sweden and the other Scandinavian countries, in terms of both teaching *about, for* and *through* democracy and active participation (Mikkelsen, 2003). In general, Scandinavian students have good knowledge of matters concerning democracy and citizenship, and express high confidence that they are able to exert influence by active engagement (Swedish National Agency for Education, 2010a). The aspects of democracy and influence that Swedish compulsory and upper secondary education have focused upon have varied

during the last fifty years, mainly along the dimensions of functional and scientific rational versus normative orientation and collective versus individual focus (cf. Englund, 1999). In addition, the attention paid to democracy and other social functions in relation to the economic functions of education has clearly varied over time. For instance, a normative conception of democracy was prominent directly after the end of World War II; school was supposed to foster citizens who could resist totalitarian ideologies and take responsibility for *'social development founded on the citizen's own insights and will'* (Ministry of Education and Ecclesiastical Affairs 1948, p. 3). Soon, however, other functions of education overshadowed its democratic objectives, which were more or less taken for granted. A functional rational view of democracy as mainly a representative form of government became prevalent in the 1950s and 1960s (Englund, 1999).

Reflecting the sharpened ideological tensions and radical left movement of the late 1960s, the need to educate committed citizens who could actively engage in and influence social life was strongly emphasised once again in the 1970 national curriculum plan for upper secondary education (Swedish National Board of Education, 1970), similar to the ideas espoused directly after the end of World War II. An objective regarded as crucial was to train children and young people to critically think and evaluate ideas, in order to avoid indoctrination.

In a democratic society where one wishes to put more responsibility on the individual human, training of the intellect is of great importance. The clarity of thinking, the ability of critical and autonomous assessment and resistance of tendentious influence, the ability to analyse, compare and summarise are qualities that particularly should be focused according to the Swedish National Board of Education (1970, p. 14).

Upper secondary education should also give the students possibilities to influence their working environment and studies. A central argument was that this would train students to take joint responsibility for social matters in the future. In the still valid 1994 national upper secondary school curriculum (Ministry of Education and Research, 1994), the dimension of individual responsibility is emphasised even more strongly, coupled with notions of individual freedom and uniqueness. The task of the school is *to encourage all pupils to discover their own uniqueness as individuals* and thereby *actively participate in social life by giving of their best.* (Ministry of Education and Research, 1994, p. 3)

Schools have an obligation to support the development of pupils into 'responsible persons who actively participate in and contribute to vocational and civic life' (Ministry of Education and Research, 1994, p. 5). In addition, all who work in school are supposed to promote democratic structures in school, and the teachers should ensure that all students *have real influence on the work methods, work structures, and educational content (ibid.*, p. 15). For example, they should plan the education together with the students, and help them to overcome difficulties they may have in expressing their viewpoints.

Students' right to influence their schools' working environment is also enshrined in Swedish work environment legislation (Swedish National Agency for Education 2004). Two arenas for student influence are regulated by law: the class council (*klassråd*), dealing with matters of common interest to the students in the class (Ministry of Education 1992), and the school conference at each school. The school conference, which must have equal representation of staff and students, is supposed to deal with matters of great importance to the students and provide an arena for information exchange and discussions between the head teacher, students and staff. The school conference should also attend to questions regarding the working environment. Notably, the Individual Programme is partially exempt from the class conference stipulations, since in this case the rules are to be applied *only to the extent to which it is practically possible* (Ministry of Education and Research 2010), due to the usually highly individualised and fragmented character of this programme's studies.

It may be added that a further step towards strengthening students' influence in upper secondary schools was taken in 1997, when local school boards with a student majority were introduced by way of experiment. Such school boards existed until 2007, albeit to a limited extent, when the new liberal school minister Jan Björklund put an end to them with the characteristic argument that students should not, by force of their being in majority, be able to decide over principals and teachers (Swedish Parliament, 2006). On the whole, matters of student democracy have not been high on the agenda of the present conservative-liberal coalition government. For example, democracy education was not mentioned at all in the 2009 reform of upper secondary education (Lundahl et al., 2010).

The Students

Despite a number of reforms over the years aiming to reduce inequalities among students, Swedish upper secondary school still remains highly divided along gender and class lines. Working class youths choose vocational programmes to a higher degree than young people from middle and upper class families, who predominantly choose academic programmes. Furthermore, vocational education and training at upper secondary level to a large extent consists of either male- or female-dominated programmes (Lidegran et al., 2006; Svensson, 2007). The class and gender differences are relatively minor among students taking the specially designed programmes, but students taking the Individual Programme are predominately working class and lower middle class youths (Svensson, 2007, p. 309).

The strong gender divisions constitute the most eye-catching aspect; in 2008/09 almost half of all male students at upper secondary level attended a national programme (or equivalent) with eighty to one hundred per cent male students (specifically the Energy, Construction, Electricity, Vehicle, Industry and Technology programmes), while sixty per cent of the girls followed a programme with seventy per cent or more female students (specifically the Child and Recreation, Business and Administration, Handicraft, Food and Health Programmes) (Swedish National Agency for Education, 2010b).

Gender differences are most pronounced among students of working-class and lower middle class backgrounds. These girls tend to choose traditional female vocational programmes and boys the male-coded vocational programmes. *The higher up we go in the social hierarchy, the closer girls and boys come in their educational choices* (Lidegran et al., 2006, p. 20) but the vocational programmes, targeting working-class students, tend still to be settings where the sexes meet to low extent (Arnman and Järnek, 2006, p. 15). Students with non-Swedish backgrounds are distributed amongst programmes in a similar pattern to the students with Swedish background, except that they are more heavily represented on the Individual Programme (Sandell, 2006; Swedish National Agency for Education, 2010b).

Even the results, in terms of grades, students' eligibility for higher education and the proportions of young people who continue to higher studies, vary according to class, gender and ethnicity. Young men tend to leave upper secondary education without complete grades to a higher extent than young women, and students from lower social strata drop-out more frequently than students from higher strata (Svensson, 2007, p. 312). Moreover, despite improvements in recent years, 40 and 50 per cent of young women and men with non-Swedish origins, respectively, do not reach the goals set for upper secondary education and obtain final grades that provide basic eligibility for higher education (Swedish National Agency for Education, 2009c, p. 23). In addition, geographical location matters. For example, students from many rural and sparsely populated municipalities do not enter higher education despite being eligible, and in certain smaller industrial municipalities less than half of the young people leave upper secondary school with complete grades (Jönsson, 2006; also see Sandell, 2007).

A further factor that may affect (and sometimes frustrate) students is that they have to select schools and programmes in an increasingly fragmented and market-oriented choice situation, often with very little help and support (Lund, 2008). Girls and students with a non-Swedish background particularly express frustration over this difficult choice situation (Dresch and Lovén, 2010), and the proportion of students who change programme after some time has increased. Twelve per cent of all students changed upper secondary school between 2007 and 2008. The level was somewhat higher for students of non-Swedish origin (Swedish National Agency for Education, 2009c, p. 207).

The patterns discussed above are well exemplified by the students taking the programmes addressed in detail in this book—the vocationally-oriented Vehicle and Child and Recreation Programmes, the academic Natural Science and Social Science Programmes, and the Individual Programme (Table 2.1).

Table 2.1. Students taking the five programmes included in the study: national statistics (2008/09).

	Natural Science	Social Science	Vehicle	Child and Recreation	Individual Programme	Upper secondary ed. (total)
Number of students	31,335	53,807	13,376	12,694	31,532	396,336
Females (%)	47	62	9	74	42	49
Students of Non-Swedish origin (%)	21	18	10	12	42	16
Accepted by their first choice (%)	88	86	73	91	70	81
Go to higher education within 3 years (%)	77.0	55.6	1.6	25.0	2.1	40.8

Source: Swedish National Agency for Education, 2010b.

The *Vehicle Programme* has ninety per cent male students, the same proportion of students of Swedish origin, and only a few per cent pursue tertiary education within three years following the programme. On the *Child and Recreation Programme* three out of four students are girls, and here too the proportion of students with a foreign background is low. Approximately twenty-five per cent continue to higher education, substantially less than the average for the whole upper secondary school cohort, but considerably more than the percentages for the Vehicle programme and most other vocational programmes. The *Natural Science Programme* has the most even gender distribution, and the highest percentage continuing to university studies—almost eight out of ten. It is also the national upper secondary programme with the highest proportion of students of non-Swedish origin—more than twenty per cent. Girls constitute more than sixty per cent of the students on the *Social Science Programme*, and more than half of its students attend some form of tertiary level education within three years of graduation. The proportion of students of foreign background is twenty per cent, considerably higher than the average. Finally, the *Individual Programme* has a marked over-representation of young people of non-Swedish origin and a majority of boys. Only a few per cent of the students subsequently attend higher studies. However, it should be added that the students on the Individual Programme constitute a far more heterogeneous group than is commonly assumed, and a substantial proportion of them are eligible for a national programme (Swedish National Agency for Education, 2007, p. 19).

It should be noted that the majority of students on the Individual Programme are actually referred to it without having actively applied. A little more than half of these students come directly from compulsory education. The other half (ca. 11.000 students) consists of immigrant students at the IVIK (2000 students) and young people who have taken time out after compulsory school and have started their studies on the Individual programme for a second time, or have started but dropped out from a national programme (around 9.000 students in all). In a report from the Swedish National Agency for Education (2007) it is thus concluded that 'Students on the Individual programmes cannot just be characterised as 'ineligible', 'unmotivated' or 'new Swedes', but also 'the dropouts', 'the swappers' and 'the waiting ones'' (*ibid.*, p. 5), reflecting that there are a multitude of motives for attending the Individual Programme.

Final comments

It is very easy to characterise the Swedish *gymnasieskola* as being under strong neo-liberal influence, given the profoundly radical (by international standards) marketisation, decentralisation and emphasis on individual autonomy and entrepreneurialism. The freedom and responsibility of the individual youth to become the architect of his/her own studies and future life is accentuated as never before. One may readily assume that the major trends of individualisation, competition and performativity are also reflected in the way democracy and student influence are thought of and enacted in schools. However, responses of fourteen-year-old Swedish students reported in the 2009 International *Civic and Citizenship Education Study* (Swedish National Agency for Education, 2010c) indicate that such a perception would be too one-dimensional and simplistic.

Almost eighty per cent of the students indicated that their teachers pay attention to their opinions. Nearly a third of the students report that they had tried to influence conditions in school (mainly regarding school meals, the teaching situation, the physical and social environment) within the preceding year (*ibid.*, p. 101). Further, perhaps most encouragingly, a large majority were in favour of student influence, and had a positive opinion about the value of collective organisation. Four out of five students believed that groups of students can contribute to problem-solving in school, and even more assumed that students' participation may improve schools. Furthermore, almost nine out of ten students believed that collective student action has more influence than individual action (*ibid.*, p. 109). Central questions considered in the following chapters are whether (and if so to what extent) such ideas are supported and enacted in the examined settings.

Chapter 3

The empirical study

Dennis Beach and Elisabet Öhrn

Choice of programmes and schools

As pointed out in chapter two, there are some obvious similarities between Swedish upper secondary programmes. All programmes except the Individual Programme are three years long, all have common core subjects and all can provide matriculation requirements for entry to higher education. However, there are also some important differences between vocational and academic programmes related to gender and social class, and between schools in different municipalities in terms of both class and ethnicity. In accordance with our intention to cover such variations in the project, we have researched both vocational and academic programmes, in both traditionally male domains and traditionally female domains, offered in schools based in several regions.

The researched programmes from the academic domain are the Natural Science Programme and the Social Science Programme. Both of these programmes are traditionally high-status programmes, and nowadays similar proportions of students attend them; in 2008/2009 almost fifty per cent of the students attending the Natural Sciences Programme were young women, and the corresponding figure for the Social Science Programme was a little more than sixty per cent (Swedish National Agency for Education, 2010b).

From the vocational domain we have included the Vehicle Programme and the Child and Recreation Programme. Students of both of these programmes are, like those of Swedish vocational programmes in general, highly divided with respect to gender; young women accounted for slightly less than 10 per cent of students attending the Vehicle Programme, but almost 75 per cent of those attending the Child and Recreation Programme in 2008/2009 (Swedish National Agency for Education, 2010b). We have also included the Individual Programme. A little more than forty per cent of the national intake of this programme is currently women (ibid, see also chapter two).

The programmes, and their students, have been investigated at three public-sector upper secondary schools, each of which is fairly large (hosting about

1500-2000 students) and offers all or almost all of the national programmes. The schools are located in different parts of Sweden and although there are some demographic and socio-economic differences between them, they have not been chosen to represent any specific demographic and socio-economic structures. This would prove difficult as upper secondary schools generally have large catchment areas and unlike secondary schools they do not mostly recruit from the local neighbourhood. The names used for the schools are anonymised.

The first of the schools, Ulmus School, is located in a medium-sized Swedish university town. The educational standard in the town is quite high in relation to the national average and the proportion of people who are in unskilled work and lack formal educational qualifications above secondary level is very low. The proportion of twenty-year-olds who have attained general admission standards for higher education is greater than the national average. However, these differences are not reflected in terms of income, since the income level of the population in the region matches national averages. The number of residents (aged 16-64) born outside the Scandinavian countries also matches the national average. The school is exposed to competition due to the relatively high number of independent upper-secondary schools located in the town or close to it.

The second school, Apel School, is located in a small Swedish town, in which there is no institute of higher education but two universities and one university of technology are accessible in two neighbouring towns some thirty and forty miles away. The educational level of the population in the town is similar to the national average, as are income levels and the proportions of low skilled workers in the workforce, twenty-year-olds who have attained general admission requirements for higher education and foreign-born residents. Upper-secondary schools are not substantially exposed to competition and public choice effects in the town, as no independent upper-secondary schools are located in it.

The third school, Currant Upper Secondary School, is located in a medium-sized Swedish town. In the town there is a campus where higher education in subjects related to care, education and technology is available. Three universities and one university of technology are accessible in three neighbouring cities some fifty miles away. The educational level of the population in the town, income levels, and the proportions of low skilled workers in the workforce, twenty-year-olds who have attained general admission requirements for higher education and foreign-born residents are all similar to national averages. The school is substantially exposed to competition due to a relatively high number of independent upper-secondary schools in the town or close to it. However, the independent upper-secondary schools do not run any Individual programmes (which were the programmes researched in Currant Upper Secondary School).

Ethnography

To explore the conditions of the above programmes, and the students' experiences of schooling in them, we have used an approach to ethnography that is commonly found in Scandinavian educational research. The general aim of this approach is to develop theoretical and practical descriptions of education lives, identities and activities through detailed, situated investigations that produce knowledge about the basic conditions of education systems, practices and set-ups, the participants' perspectives and the latent meanings of education contexts. This knowledge is then synthesised to 'ground' research accounts and expand ideas about the matters addressed (Gordon, Lahelma and Beach, 2003; Gordon, Hynninen, Lahelma, Metso, Palmu and Tolonen, 2006; Larsson, 2006).

In our research foreshadowed questions of the education field, as outlined in chapter one, related to democratic education/learning framed the initial foci and gave direction to the research. However, the subsequent data production and analysis developed from multiple sources and perspectives, with some randomisation, in order to allow the identification and development of previously unexplored dimensions of education interchanges without potential over-steering by 'pet-ideas' and concepts (Trondman, 2008). This is a general ethnographic aim, to avoid hindering the emergence of original or surprising elements in the research (Beach, 2010). Once they have been formed, the established ideas have been explored and tested in terms of their general scope against further data as a basis for the possible development and refinement of ethnographic theory. This included continuous joint discussion and analyses, and although we cannot claim to have carried out a collective ethnography, as described by Gordon et al. (2006), our work does bear some resemblance to theirs with respect to the development of joint foci and themes.

Three main principles have guided our work that have also been described by Jeffrey and Troman (2004), that research should ideally take place over an extended and well-organised time period in order:

- To allow a fuller range of empirical situations and transitions to be observed and analysed and to allow for the emergence of contradictory behaviours and perspectives;
- To allow for continuous reflections concerning the complexity of human

contexts and the relations between the appropriate cultural, political and
social levels of the research site and individual and group agency there;

- To include explicit theoretical perspectives in order to sensitise field
research and analysis and provide an opportunity to use empirical data for
the interrogation of macro and middle range theories and to develop (or
ground) new ideas.

The analysis adopted by the researchers in relation to these questions has
been of an abductive character, of a kind used in (or similar to) the constant
comparative method of grounded theorising. This is a common analytical
approach in ethnography that has been extensively described in research
methods books such as those by Hammersley and Atkinson (2007) and Burgess
(1995). Both closeness and analytical distance are important. Close, detailed
descriptions of activities are obtained through participant observation, while
analytical distance is provided by the use of scientifically generated theories,
which are also challenged by empirical variations and modified in the encounter
with the field. There is a dialectical relationship between theory and empirical
data in this respect (Trondman, 2008).

The fieldwork

The project involved three field researchers, each of whom observed and
interviewed two groups of participants. One sub-study researched one class
taking the academic Natural Science Programme, and a second sub-study
researched the traditionally female vocational Child and Recreation Programme.
These sub-studies were conducted by Carina Hjelmér and they are presented
in chapters four and five. A third sub-study investigated the academic Social
Science Programme and a fourth the traditionally male vocational Vehicle
Programme. These sub-studies were conducted by Per-Åke Rosvall and are
presented in chapters six and seven. The fifth sub-study researched two classes
from an Individual Programme. These investigations were conducted by
Marianne Dovemark and are presented in chapter eight.

In each context both the content and organisation of the education were
in focus, allowing us to identify a number of important issues concerning
schooling and school experiences related to democracy and various dimensions
of democratic learning. As for the content and form of teaching, gender theory
perspectives suggested that we should be concerned with identifying and
focusing on the understanding of democracy and the presentation(s) of the
political subject (Arnot and Dillabough, 2000; Arnot, 2006). As suggested

by Davies (1994), these matters might involve, for instance, focusing on direct teaching about rights, direct consciousness raising and active listening to student questions. As suggested by Gordon (2006), the distinction between education for future or present citizenship and participation may also be deemed interesting.

In order to capture student initiatives and responses, the observations have focused on students' acts in relation to issues of democracy and attempts to exert influence in the classroom and the wider school context. These efforts have included focusing on youth's targets for change and the process of negotiation.

The fieldwork in each of the settings researched included conversations with staff and students. In addition, we have carried out formal individual interviews with a selection of teachers and both formal individual and group interviews with the students in all the classes and groups. These have included conversations about the processes observed, the students' images of their respective schools' messages regarding their rights and obligations of democratic participation, how they see their opportunities and how they act with respect to these issues. They have also included questions about young people's experiences of their impact in various informal and formal contexts in and outside school. Here we included questions about their social and political participation outside the school and their vision for the future regarding such participation. The importance of life outside formal institutions is often emphasised in gender theory research. This appears to be particularly important given research showing the existence of informal, critical challenges to the formal school's understanding in alternative citizenship discourses (Reay and Mirza, 1997; Sernhede, 2007).

The project has thus provided opportunities to relate school processes and experiences to the understanding, commitments and actions of students. In this manner it may contribute to theoretical knowledge about the importance of contingent and contextual factors for democratic participation in institutional practices as well as to practical knowledge about how to develop democratic education in schools. When conducting our research we have followed established ethical conventions (see e.g. www.codex.vr.se; Beach, 1999c). Participants have been fully informed about the project, including methods and forms of publication in writing, and of their right to withdraw at any time. Information about contact addresses was also provided and participants were informed that the materials produced would only be used by research personnel. All field materials were to be safety-code-stored.

Chapter 4

Collective actions in the Natural Science Programme

Carina Hjelmér

Introduction

This chapter is about collective actions of students in a first-year Natural Science class consisting of sixteen boys and fourteen girls at Ulmus School. It is based on data from one year of ethnographical fieldwork, including participant observations and interviews with the students, the teachers and the head teacher. This data consists of field notes from eighty-five days in this class covering one hundred and forty-five lessons (including thirty mathematics lessons) and fifteen class meetings. It was produced through participant observation. In addition I have conducted ten group interviews with twenty-eight students (fourteen girls and fourteen boys), one group interview with five teachers, one individual interview with one teacher and one individual interview with the headteacher. The interviews were carried out during the spring term 2009.

According to the Swedish national curriculum for upper secondary, post-compulsory education (Lpf 94), schools should not only teach students about democracy, but also ensure that they 'live democracy' by having real influence on the educational organisation, methods and contents (Ministry of Education and Research, 1994; see chapter two in this book). This chapter considers the latter aspect; how democracy is 'lived' in daily school life. During the fieldwork year there were several situations in which students influenced minor matters, but they are only briefly described. Instead, the chapter mainly addresses one of few more profound and illuminating incidents with regard to student influence, since it embraced a critique of teaching, involved the whole class, and was prolonged. The action concerned the pace, difficulty level, and marking in mathematics. Of special interest is *the process* of the students' attempt to exert influence (who was involved, about what, and what resources were used), *the responses* of the teachers and head teacher, and *the results* of the students' action.

Background

In their analysis of Swedish upper secondary school, Broady and Börjesson (2006) conclude that the Natural Science Programme has had high status, especially since the 1990s. Students enrolled on this programme generally have substantial cultural and social capital (Bourdieu, 1994; Broady, Börjesson, Bertilsson, Larsson, Lidegran and Nordqvist, 2009), come from homes with well-educated parents, and obtained the highest marks in lower secondary school (Broady and Börjesson, 2006). Furthermore, since the 1990s the Natural Science Programme has had more equal proportions of male and female students than any other upper secondary school programme (Lidegran, Börjesson, Nordqvist and Broady, 2006).

According to interviews with students from all kinds of programmes reported by Lidegran et al. (2006), attending a mixed gender programme gave the highest status, hence this will have boosted the esteem of the Natural Science Programme, and its students. These general features of the programme, and the national cohort of students taking it, correspond well to the class studied here. The students (and teachers, including the head) talked about the Natural Science Programme being for the clever ones, and that it could be very tough to get high marks because of the high performance of everyone in the class. Expectations of hard work and high performance were general features in all subjects, including arts and sports. Other features shared by students of this class and those interviewed by Lidegran et al. (2006) were that their parents generally have similar economic and social positions (e.g. the mother may be a surgeon and the father a medical superintendent), and they spent time outside school hours in mixed gender groups. Four of the students in the class investigated here have an immigrant background.

The education at Ulmus School in general, and not least in the Natural Science Programme, was characterised by strong classification (Bernstein, 2000). Although vocational and academic programmes were based in the same building, there were distinct borders between them. For example, they were based in different parts of the building, and during breaks the students mingled with those from the same kind of programme. Every class had its own home classroom, where they had most of their lessons, with some exceptions, e.g. for art and physical education. Moreover, even if some of the teachers were qualified to teach in both vocationally and academically-oriented programmes they rarely did (cf. Johansson, 2009), and none of the teachers who taught the class addressed in this study were involved in vocational programmes. A year prior to the study, the teachers had been reorganised into cross-disciplinary teams with joint responsibility for each class, which could be interpreted as a weakening of subject boundaries (Bernstein, 2000). However, all of the teachers remained members of specific subject teams.

The Natural Science Programme was also characterised by strong framing, as defined by Bernstein (2000). Generally, the teachers controlled the teaching, and all of the students had to stay in the classroom for the whole lesson, with only a few exceptions at the end of the school year. The educational methods used were decided by the teachers, and clear, distinct guidelines were issued even for autonomous student work. Broady et al. (2009) argue that Natural Science is the programme that has been least influenced by pedagogical innovation. They also observed, similarly to the results in this study, that the Natural Science students were pleased with this allegedly effective way of learning in which the teachers, 'the experts', told them what to do. Pacing and use of time were also strongly regulated. For example, in the autumn term the class had a fully booked timetable with long days at school and short breaks between lessons. In addition, the students often had homework and many examinations. It was extremely uncommon for lesson times to be reduced, or even for students to ask for reductions, and almost all of the students arrived punctually in the mornings.

Formal and informal influence

The school has a common students' council, with preferably two representatives from each class. The council meetings, announced two weeks in advance, were supposed to be preceded by formal class councils with a chair and a secretary. The matters raised by the class were supposed to be brought up at the students' council meetings by the class representatives. However, during this year of field study, there were only two meetings, one of which I attended. The students did not appear to take the meeting seriously and, as observed in other studies, neither the teachers (including the head), nor the students, seemed to regard the students' council as important (Danell, Klerfelt, Runevad and Trodden, 1999; Öhrn, 2005; Kamperin, 2005a). In the investigated Natural Science class, only one student, a boy, was interested in participating in the students' council. The other students said they thought that joining the council would be a waste of time needed for study-related activities, such as lessons and homework. In addition, every class at Ulmus School has one hour a week scheduled, the so-called class hour, in which students and teachers can (for example) raise current issues for discussion. However, the class hours scheduled for the Natural Science class were also used for getting information from the class teachers, having a cup of coffee and playing games, organised by the students. Finally, the head teacher had planned to establish an 'N-council' (Natural Science council), with two students from each of the six classes, three teachers and herself, to increase the students' involvement in the programme, but the plans were not realised during the field year.

The students were also often invited to influence minor matters concerning working methods and content informally, within terms of reference set by the teacher. For example, the students could decide the order of some content in the course, or the day that the next test should take place. Dovemark (2004a) argues that this kind of direct influence in agreement between students and teachers, also observed in studies by Öhrn (2004) and Kamperin (2005a), is a limited way of exercising influence, and increasingly individualised. In this Natural Science class students rarely raised critique, and on these rare occasions, the students nearly always yielded immediately if the response from the teacher was negative. Several students expressed anxiety that their marks may be reduced if they complained too much. Given this context, the collective action regarding their mathematics lessons analysed in this chapter appears to have been highly unusual.

The teaching situation in mathematics

The students found the start of their upper secondary school programme tough on the whole, and maths to be the most arduous subject. The teaching situation was characterised by visible pedagogy (Bernstein, 1990), a context of reproduction with hierarchic teacher-student relations, and strong pacing following strict sequencing rules both during lessons and in homework. For instance, the teacher always started the lessons with a few minutes of briefing at the whiteboard, going through examples taken directly from the textbook, then the students had to solve related tasks in the textbook, while the teacher walked around guiding those who asked for help (cf. Beach, 1999a; Lundin, 2008). All students, even the highest-achievers, needed to work on maths at home almost daily and during weekends to keep up. This situation favoured students with well-educated parents, i.e. those with high cultural capital at home. In addition, many of the students in this class also helped each other tackle tasks at home via an internet community. The community, initiated by the students, provided support in what the students described as a give and take manner, and they were very pleased with the results. In this way, they increased their already high cultural capital (Bourdieu, 1994).

The highly performance-related teaching situation was permeated with competition, which was expressed in various ways. For example, the teacher continuously showed the students a list indicating exactly what each student needed to do to improve his/her marks for the next test, and many students talked about the stress caused by the risk of low marks. This in turn led to comparisons between the students, and several boys (especially) loudly compared their results. Connell (2002) shows that such competitive patterns are common among boys, but are also related to social background and local gender regimes. Working class boys observed in the cited study generally competed by fighting, while boys at elite schools were competitive in ways the school supported, like the boys in this class, which in turn often resulted in high achievement in school. Furthermore, stress was raised by the need for help, and the ways in which it was addressed, in the maths lessons. More often than not, many of the students and the teacher worked even during the breaks, but there were about five students who had not received help from the teacher despite asking for it. Of those who regularly asked for and received help, about half of the class, a majority were girls who achieved highly in tests. The teacher confirmed that this had been the common situation in the Natural Science Programme in recent years. Accordingly, Arnot and Reay observed that high-achieving middle-class girls used the most appropriate pedagogic language and displayed the greatest emotional competence when relating to teachers. Consequently, they were listened to more, and had greater influence over their learning, than the other students (Arnot and Reay, 2004; Arnot, 2006).

However, there were many students, also from middle-class homes, who almost never asked for help, even when they did not understand how to solve the problems. Two girls from this group, who usually talked in front of the class regarding other school matters, expressed their feelings in that kind of situation as follows:

Marion: When he [the teacher] has his briefings he only says 'But do you understand? Yes, good, then you can start working now'. He takes it for granted that we should know so much already, and if you ask about something when he walks around, all that happens is [the teacher asks]: 'But, what is 40,000 multiplied by 7' (strong, rather brusque voice)? Then you just 'Er, I don't know' (weak and feeble voice). Then he completes the task for you, but you still don't understand. It's so silly!

Irene: Yes, he always does the task for you so you don't understand; no, he's not good at explaining.   (Group interview, March 2009)

The girls felt uncomfortable and silly, not understanding the things the teacher asked about, and did not seem to have the appropriate language to communicate their feelings or need for help. In this kind of performance-related and competitive practice, the first objective is to rank and divide the students (Beach, 1999a), focusing attention on the highest performers an aspect the girls quoted implicitly expressed. Marion and Irene also describe how this mode of teaching does not make them understand how to do the tasks, and does not fit their way of learning. As is evident in Beach's research on mathematics education at upper secondary school, students' understandings are always subordinated to other goals, such as getting the course done or working through the book. He argues that the repetitive way of teaching mathematics rewards students who in addition to having some 'mathematical talent' can subordinate themselves to working hard and endure the boring, stereotyped working method (Beach, 1999a). To acquire the legitimate pedagogic code in mathematics in this class, it seemed to be important for the students to know about the maths they should learn and accept the teaching modes, in addition to knowing how to talk to the teacher (Bernstein, 2000).

The process of influencing

Right from the start of the autumn term the difficulties in maths were recurrent issues among the students. The atmosphere was often stressful, and even on my second day at school with this class I was told about the problematic situation in maths:

The two boys in front of me begin to talk to me during the short break. They tell me they have many scheduled lessons every week. One of them tells me there is one thing I can write about in my book, and that is about the far too fast pace in maths. It is very fast all the time. A new item every day, and when they do not get all the tasks done during the lesson they fall immediately behind if they cannot do it at home the same day. They finish the conversation by saying 'So please, write in your book that maths is tough and advances far too rapidly'.   (Field notes, August 2008)

Above all, the students talked about the briefings being too short and difficult, the pace of learning being too rapid, the textbook and the examinations being too difficult (and much more difficult than those used in the same course in other programmes, which could lead to unfair marking). Almost all of the students engaged in the discussions during breaks, and even though there were differences about getting help from the teacher and results of tests, they all seemed to agree about the unreasonable demands in maths and the need for them to act.

During the breaks, the students repeatedly discussed and shared opinions with each other in various small groups. Like the students observed in Öhrn's (1998) study, the students in this Natural Science class obtained a joint understanding of the situation through these discussions, identified possible strategies for action, and became able to take collective action. Relating to previous research, the Natural Science students' discussion about the importance of being a big, strong group when pursuing the issues about mathematics appears to be rather unusual. For example, some studies indicate that such collective strategies are mostly favoured by working-class groups (Öhrn, 2005), and more generally recent developments in schools have shifted emphasis from collective actions to autonomy and individualism (Gordon, 2006). However, the students in this class made clear that these kinds of collective actions would only be seriously considered in situations that specifically concerned issues of importance for themselves, and not (for example) in long-term work in the students' council.

After two weeks of internal discussions, the students agreed that the best way to act was to describe the problems rationally in conversation with the class teachers. This is consistent with observations in previous studies that conversing with teachers (and ultimately the head teacher) is a common strategy to tackle problems, and the willingness and listening competence of teachers are crucial for positive results (Öhrn, 2004; Kamperin, 2005b). In addition, the students decided to talk to their parents at home about these problems (see also Öhrn, 1998, 2005; Kamperin, 2005a). According to the students, many of the parents talked to the class teachers during the regular parents-teacher meeting soon after about their children's complaints and described how much of their leisure time they had to use for maths homework. The class teachers and the parents agreed that something needed to be done and the class teachers promised to help the students to talk to the maths teacher.

During the next class hour, the class teachers and the whole class discussed the mathematics situation. The class teachers told the students that often the best way to tackle such problems is for students to talk to teachers themselves and describe the problems. One of the teachers suggested that they should elect a small group who could represent the class when trying to find a solution together with the maths teacher because 'It could be hard for him to face a discussion with the whole class at the same time'. The teachers also gave recommendations about taking notes from this class hour with the intention to be rational and constructive. The class agreed that this was a good idea, and a small group consisting of one girl and one boy, Maria and Markus (who had stood out as polite and constructive on several occasions, and were not afraid of making suggestions), were elected to present the whole class' standpoints. Such approaches by 'well-behaved' students, who are appreciated by the teachers, has often proved to be a successful way for students to make teachers listen to their arguments, and hence exert influence (Öhrn, 2005).

After one of the maths lessons Maria and Markus, joined by Sanna (who was asked to come because they decided a group of three may be better), met with Bengt, the teacher. A week or so later, the class teachers and students talked about the mathematics situation again during a class hour.

> Charlie, one of the class teachers, asks 'What has happened in maths?' One of the girls answers that the students have made a help queue, writing their names on the white board, but some people still don't get help. They have also decided that if the help queue does not work the students have to help each other. Marion says that there was also a group of support teachers who could perhaps come to the class on Friday afternoons. Charlie says 'Yes, I said I could check that, but I haven't got the time at the moment'. Maria continues talking about the meeting with Bengt [the mathematics teacher] and how they talked to him about his briefings, if he could make them clearer and easier to understand, 'But he answered there are so many in this class who are very good at mathematics and it will be boring for them if they just have to sit and wait'. Markus continues 'But it is really important to find a balance in maths. We don't have the time to get help'. Karin says she has just had an idea, and suggests that the teacher could first give a briefing for everyone, then the ones who wanted could start working by themselves, while the teacher gave a more basic briefing for the rest of the class. Some of the other students agree and several, both boys and girls, talk with excited and engaged voices.
>
> ...

Charlie asks the three in the group whether Bengt listened to them. Markus says something about perhaps they were not sufficiently prepared with notes before the meeting. Maria continues by stating that Bengt said there was really pretty little that could be changed about the things they discussed; 'Changing to an easier book was not possible, nothing could be done about the pace of the education, and making the briefings in front of the white board easier wasn't possible'. Markus adds that Bengt also said there was no difference in difficulty level between the programmes, which Markus questions. Tomas agrees, and refers to his friends who are attending the Social Science Programme, saying that they are having a much easier Mathematics A course, although the maths teacher says that it should be the same degree of difficulty, which Tomas says is not true. Karin then says you are not necessarily better in maths if you are on our programme. Andrej says with a sigh 'No, you only need to look at the results of the test; half of the class only passed!' One of the class teachers sums up, 'Now we have a constructive proposal from Karin. The group could talk to the maths teacher about it'.

(Field notes, October 2008)

In the conversation cited above the students were excited and highly engaged in a constructive and polite way. In spite of the high stress level nobody talked about the teacher negatively, but presented creative and seemingly reasonable ideas about how to improve the situation. The students in the elected group took their commission seriously and blamed themselves for not being sufficiently prepared before the meeting. Marion also, in a responsible and constructive way, tried to communicate her and other students' need of extra help by referring to a previous class-hour in which the possible solution involving assistance from support teachers was raised. Such responsible and constructive behaviour was identified by both the class teachers and the head teacher in interviews as an important quality that improved the students' chances of successfully exercising influence (see also Öhrn, 1998; Arnot, 2006). Arnot argues that this is typical of the behaviour of students from middle class homes (and teachers' responses to them), that is students possessing cultural capital speak in a way that teachers understand and recognise as a polite and 'right' way to speak.

Having the scheduled class hours as regular opportunities for joint discussions involving the whole class seemed to provide an important basis for the students' collective action (Öhrn, 1998). About a third of the students were active during the discussions in the classroom, debated the same issues as in the small group discussions during breaks, and talked in a supportive way—one said something and others filled in (see also Öhrn, 1998, 2005). The students acted collectively, by one starting and others following up and deepening the arguments or added new points, thereby forming what could be called a collective construction of the problem (Skeggs, 1991). As, for example, Krantz (2005) argues, it is a fundamental democratic requirement that the students should have equal opportunities not only to voice their opinions but also to remain quiet. Field notes and interviews with the students who were quiet during these discussions indicated that their silence was self-chosen, and they were of the same opinion as those who talked.

Boys and girls in this Natural Science class acted in a seemingly similar way with joint responsibility for pursuing issues of a similar kind. The students also met teachers who, in almost all subjects, let boys and girls alternately answer when they asked questions in the classroom. When electing the small representative group, the natural choice (according to both the students and teachers) seemed to be one boy and one girl. Previous research has shown that girls tend to be the driving forces in negotiations with teachers (Öhrn, 1998; Kamperin, 2005a), but that boys dominate in communications in the classroom (Lahelma and Öhrn, 2003).

However, good social cohesiveness and organisation appear to be more important than the sex of the students for students' possibilities to pursue issues (Öhrn, 1998) and to establish positions of influence (Gordon, Holland and Lahelma, 2000). The students in this class attend one of the most equally gender-mixed programmes, which (as mentioned above) gives high status at upper secondary school (Lidegran et al., 2006). As observed in the top set groups in a study by Holm and Öhrn (2007), cross-gender networking among these students gave them the strength to speak up in the classroom. Furthermore, many of the students in this class of both sexes seemed to be purposeful and rational, and faced with a teaching situation that was experienced as unfair and strenuous they all had something to gain by taking joint responsibility for the action. As Thorne (1993) argues, gender constructions can differ depending on circumstances; they may appear in some situations, and be ignored, disregarded or radically changed in others, among the same group of students.

When interviewed, many of the students talked about the difficulties in making an impact when criticising a teachers' teaching, and they emphasised the importance of adults giving the students' arguments and claims legitimacy.

Nevertheless, it is also important for teachers to 'foster democracy', by supporting and educating the students to be politically aware in terms of the various options and strategies that could be adopted (Öhrn, 2005). In line with the representative democratic model, the class teachers in this Natural Science class instructed the students how to continue their actions by discussions in class hours, and electing a small representative group. However, the teachers' intentions appear to have been ambiguous; they seem to have wanted to give the students possibilities to act and exert influence via the elected group, but also to avoid rebellious action against the adults' norms, and for the students to communicate responsibly, with concern for the teacher's feelings (see Denvall, 1999 for similar observations). When the group reported their failed negotiations there were no further instructions from the teachers, who instead suggested that the group have a new meeting with Bengt, which never took place. Even if the class in this study were disappointed about the negative result, several students told me that they found this way of acting enlightening, and had learned something they could apply in future conflicts (see also Aldersson, 2000; Öhrn, 2005).

Responses from adults

The mathematics teacher told the students that their demands could not result in any changes, because mathematics has to be taught in a specific way, step by step in a predetermined order. This characterisation of mathematics education is current not only in Sweden, but also internationally (e.g. Namukasa, 2004; Lundin, 2008; Pellegrino and Goldman, 2008).

> Well, now it is a fact that maths is not suitable to be influenced by students, because they need to have all these building blocks to carry out the next steps. So it is impossible for them to choose anything.
>
> (Bengt, group interview, April 2009)

Most of the other teachers in the team expressed the same view about mathematics in the interviews. For example, Britta, the English teacher, described how the students in her subject could choose between some items in the course and concluded, 'Because I don't need to manage the course like in maths, in exactly the same order and everything, it doesn't need to fit together all the time'. Arne, the social studies teacher, added some critical thoughts about how the team had handled student influence. However, he concluded, 'But I can really understand your problem Bengt, you cannot choose content in maths'.

The head teacher took the same stance about mathematics' distinct position when she was consulted by the class teachers in late October, since the students were still discontented. However, in contrast to a situation observed by Kamperin (2005b), where the students obtained support from the head teacher, the head teacher here acted more as a support for the mathematics teacher. She decided to have a meeting in the middle of November with the whole class, Bengt, and the two class teachers 'So we get the same picture'. Moreover, she had contact with the class teachers and the maths teacher, but not with the students either before or after the meeting. Clearly, therefore, the head teacher did not endeavour to alter the power imbalance in favour of the students, a key factor, according to Denvall (1999), for intervention by the head to be a beneficial resource for students. In her view, her responsibility was to listen to the teachers and to inform the students about their conclusions.

There is a parallel here to Bertilsson's (2007) study, where teachers of natural science subjects could influence their working situation and obtain higher status in the school leaders' eyes more easily than other teachers. The head teacher described Bengt's elucidation at the meeting as very proficient, and her confidence in his handling of the situation in turn influenced her own participation.

> *Carina*: If you look at your role in all this, how would you describe it?
> *Gunnel*: My role is to listen. Thus I think it is like this, it would have been very difficult if I had not got reassurance from the teacher that it is going to go very well, do you understand? The teacher's judgement was; there is discontent now, but this will end very well and nobody in the class is going to fail and so on. (Interview, May 2009)

However, even if the great majority of the teachers seemed to have the same opinion about mathematics, there was one, Kim, who held critical views.

> Kim also talks about being disappointed that nothing at all had been done to meet the students' claims, so the problems had not been solved and nothing had changed. (---) Kim talks about the problems and difficulties in situations when talking to a colleague about his or her work 'It is tremendously delicate to question a colleague', but s/he implies that it depends a little on your relationship with the colleague in question.
> (Field-notes, conversation)

It seems to be difficult to raise critical questions about a colleagues' teaching, and from one perspective it seems to depend on the kind of relationship the two teachers have. Hence, if a teacher meets a group of students whom s/he really thinks have reasonable arguments related to a colleagues' teaching, s/he may still choose to keep quiet even if s/he believes it is a difficult ethical issue (Colnerud, 1995). The tradition at this school does not seem to support critical exchange between teachers either, as one of the class teachers explained during one of the class-hours when a student asked the class teachers for help:

> The usual procedure in this school is: at first the students try [to raise issues and/or change things] themselves, and second, if that doesn't work it's the head's job. It's not the class teacher's job to talk to his/her colleague. The idea is not that we two [class teachers] should act as messengers.
>
> (Field notes, October 2008)

In the Natural Science Programme, where the classification of education is strong, with clear and distinct borders between the teachers of different subjects (Bernstein, 2000), neither colleagues nor the head seem to criticise or discuss each others' teaching. This demarcation and respect appears to be especially pronounced for maths and natural science subjects (and teachers of these subjects).

> ... Kim also says, when it comes to natural science competence there are special problems; the teacher can always resort to saying, 'You others don't know anything about this subject and you don't know anything about how we are thinking and what we must teach'.
>
> (Field-notes, conversation)

The impression from the above conversation is that maths has high status in upper secondary school (cf. Broady et al., 2009). Mathematics at Ulmus School seems to be both strongly classified with highly specialised contents, and strongly framed with strict sequencing and pacing rules (Bernstein, 2000). These conditions give the teacher the power to make unchallenged statements (which he completely believes) that there is only one way to teach mathematics properly. In this way the mathematics teacher, consciously or not, raises defences against the possibility of weakening the insulation by the students' demands.

This in turn renders attempts to criticise and exert influence very difficult (Bernstein, 2000).

The higher demands in upper secondary school compared to those in compulsory school, and the students' immaturity when starting upper secondary school, were factors the teachers often talked about, and also emphasised in the group interview.

> *Bengt*: ... I talked to some of them, but when they found out that I couldn't change anything, and that was when they still thought they could duck out of the job. That is what I mean, their aim was to avoid work. That attitude hasn't been present in the B-course, where they have simply tried to do the work.
> *Jessica*: Mm, but wasn't much of it [the discontent] due to them not understanding the demands in the upper secondary school? And now they have learned to come up to the teachers' expectations...
>
> (Group interview, April 2009)

Even if it is generally argued that upper secondary school has high demands, the Natural Science Programme appears to be especially demanding (Broady and Börjesson, 2006; Broady et al., 2009). The norm of the Natural Science student as high achieving and hard working sharply contrasts with the students' demands for a slower pace and lower difficulty level in mathematics. Hence, even if the students possessed cultural capital and used various resources that had helped in other situations; they had not learned the pedagogical code of the Natural Science Programme as a whole. For example, the students seemed highly informed about the regulative discourse (e.g. conduct, character and manner), but knew less about the instructional discourse, (e.g. selection, sequence, pacing and criteria of knowledge) (Bernstein, 2000). From this perspective, the main task of the teachers (including the head teacher) in this Natural Science class was to teach the students the right attitudes to studies, that is to become hard working, high-achievers who aim to pursue higher studies and rise to high professional positions in the future.

Results of the attempts to exert influence

No changes resulted from the students' demands for reductions in the pace and difficulty level, an easier textbook, and more equal marking between the programmes. However, some small improvements were made to satisfy the need for help. For example, the students initiated and wrote a help queue on the white board. They were also encouraged by the teacher to help each other more than before. Again these students with high cultural capital could clearly further enhance their capital by helping each other (Bourdieu, 1994).

After the meeting with the head teacher, the students seemed to be more or less resigned to the situation and stopped their collective action, although most of them still believed that no improvements had been made. They told me they had exhausted all the possibilities they could think of. Many of the students also seemed to have learned the dominant pedagogic code of this upper secondary school, and although a great majority of the students still had the same opinion about the mathematics teaching situation, i.e. that it was too arduous, they seemed to have accepted the teachers' and head teacher's arguments.

> *Robin*: In maths we just have to accept that we have to do a lot in maths.
> *Andrej and Jonas*: Yes.
> *Robin*: We must just do it anyway so ...
> *Markus*: Yes (sigh), you have to take it if you choose a programme like this. (---)
> *Carina*: So you think it's easier now?
> *Andrej*: No, not me in any case, I still think it's hard. It's more you just get used to it, that this is the way it must be.
>
> (Group interview, March 2009)

The two students quoted in the extract below seem to have learned that it is difficult to criticise a teacher's teaching successfully (cf. Öhrn, 1998), and that it is impossible to reduce the pace and difficulty of the content in a programme like this (Broady et al., 2009). When addressing these kinds of arguments, the teacher also adopted a defensive position when they talked about the marks, which for these students is the most important issue of all.

> *Anders*: I think we probably pushed the wrong things, when we said that we wanted to have easier lessons and an easier textbook, and in our programme ...
> *Electra*: I agree, that really made him defend himself and his teaching very strongly. We should have pushed the fact that we are not getting equal

marking, compared with students on the Social Science Programme, for example. (Group interview, March 2009)

The students in this class had learned that they needed this kind of mathematics to be taught in this way to be high-achieving, even if it was not ideal in all respects. Moreover, this kind of traditional, visible pedagogy (Bernstein, 2000) is the kind of teaching the students on the Natural Science Programme usually recognise as the best way of teaching (Broady et al., 2009). In addition, recognition rules refer to power relations, which in this case enabled the students to have power through the possibilities (provided by using the selected textbook, at the pace and difficulty level stipulated by the teacher) to succeed in their future studies (Bernstein, 2000).

However, even if most of the students in the class seemed to have accepted the adults' arguments about mathematics, other opinions emerged in the interviews, such as those expressed by the high-achieving girls in the interview below.

> *Julia*: I still don't think the briefings are good; it's like it's not in context. Now it's like we sit and do a sort of 'empty exercise' with no connection to anything to show how to use it at all.
> *Therese*: Yes, I totally agree.
> *Julia*: Now he is only reading the examples from the book, he is doing exactly the same thing that is already described in the book.
> *Therese*: Yes, and you can read that for yourself.
> *Julia*: So I think he should describe and explain examples in his own words instead, then I think it could also be easier for us to do it. (---)
> *Julia*: In lower secondary school we had a very competent teacher, and it felt as if he really wanted us to understand what we were doing. But now it's more like that doesn't matter, 'You just have to do the work!' (---)
> *Carina*: Is this something you can talk about?
> *Julia*: No way, he is so definite and does not listen at all, so I don't dare say anything about it.
> *Therese*: No, no. (Group interview, March 2009)

Different framing principles yield different experiences, which in turn influence what is possible to think and do (Bernstein, 1990). The girls above have experience of another way of teaching mathematics and hence are able to challenge the strong classification and framing in their maths lessons, but only silently. The marked hierarchy and strong framing of the maths lessons made these two girls feel afraid of questioning the teaching (Bernstein, 2000).

Interestingly, the critique expressed by Therese and Julia in the above example is in line with results of previous studies focused on democracy and mathematics education, which seriously challenge 'the only truth' about mathematics expressed by the teachers and head teacher in this study (e.g. Skovsmose, 1998; Vithal, 1999; Ball, Goffney and Bass, 2005; Christiansen, 2008). In other words, the power in the strong classification in mathematics at this school is not only about what is inside the subject mathematics, but also about the power relation, space and insulation between mathematics and other subjects.

Another effect of the rejection of the students' collective demands for change is that they gradually turned into individual mathematics problems for some students. In other words, it was up to the students to work harder if they wanted to get high marks, and this supposedly had nothing to do with the way of teaching. As highlighted by Gordon (2006), there is a strong general focus on individualism and autonomy in schools today, rather than on collective actions, and such a focus can be clearly discerned in this case. For example, the collectiveness and cooperation of the students' action were not praised, but rather the achievements of the individuals were emphasised. Some individual alternatives were also recommended for those who thought they needed extra support, such as joining the homework help sessions that the school provided, at fixed times outside the set timetable, or having special tuition in mathematics instead of the original lessons. However, according to some of the students who tried these solutions, they were difficult to carry through in a workable way, for example, because of the full working schedule.

Concluding remarks

In the collective action explored in this chapter, the students used methods and resources that previous experience and research have shown to be useful. However, students' possibilities to influence school matters also depend on how close their demands are to the core of school content and values (Öhrn, 1998). In this action, the students' critique concerned the maths teacher's way of handling the content and teaching, which is clearly a core issue. Moreover, the analysis shows that it is not sufficient in the Natural Science Programme to be a 'well-behaved' student who knows how to communicate with teachers (the regulative discourse). They also have to incorporate and accept an instructional discourse, defining the selection, sequence, pacing and criteria needed to be a high-achieving student (Bernstein, 2000). The entire collective of adults in school took responsibility to teach these students what is required to be a high-achieving student. It should be noted that the programme not only attracts boys and girls from the cultural elite, it also forms the future elite of the society (Broady and Börjesson, 2006).

From the beginning, boys and girls, both high-achieving and low-achieving, took a joint action that was collectively prepared. However, the visible pedagogy with strong classification and framing in mathematics (Bernstein, 2000) made it almost impossible to change the teaching. Even the high-achieving students, mostly girls, who had some influence over their own learning via the teachers' help during lessons, only had an impact as long as they followed the teacher's strong framing rules. Consequently, the students instead had to alter themselves, by working harder in school and at home, helping each other even more or using the school's extra homework help. The schools' focus on individualism and autonomy (Gordon, 2006) seemed to hinder the students' collective action. Moreover, most of the students also accepted the adults' rhetoric about mathematics education, even though they thought the problems still remained, that is they learned the legitimate pedagogic code in this performance-based school.

To some extent, the students were encouraged to be active agents, for example, during the joint discussions in class hours, and when electing the representative group to talk with the maths teacher. Even if the action did not lead to any concrete result, they still learned skills about how to act. However, the teachers' intentions regarding the students' influence appear to have been ambiguous; they seemed to want to give the students possibilities to act and exert influence, but there seemed to be underlying objectives to avoid rebellious action against the adults' norms (cf. Denvall, 1999). Gordon (2006) highlights the problematic tensions between emancipation and regulation when students try to act at school, and argues that the rights of students to be agentic are curtailed, whilst the need for their individual responsibility and achievement is stressed.

In this Natural Science class the students above all learned what is needed to *become* an adult citizen via hard work and achievement, how to *act like* responsible adult citizens who show consideration for the maths teachers' feelings when talking to him, whilst possibilities to *act citizenship* in the present were limited (Gordon, 2006). In this class, adaption to the school system seemed to be the price these Natural Science students had to pay to secure their status and future possibilities in studies and society.

Chapter 5

Negotiations in the Child and Recreation Programme

Carina Hjelmér

Introduction

This chapter is about first-year students' negotiations concerning their education in the Child and Recreation Programme at Ulmus School, the same upper secondary school that hosted the Natural Science class discussed in the previous chapter. It is also based on data from one year of ethnographical fieldwork with participant observations and interviews with the students, the teachers and the head teacher, and focuses on how 'democracy was lived' in the daily life of the school.

During this year there were several situations where students influenced minor matters, which are briefly described. However, the main focus is on negotiations that are of special interest because students, parents, teachers and the head teacher were all involved. Furthermore, the process and its results are typical and illuminative for the daily and more individual negotiations that affected the whole group of students. The negotiations concerned the pace, difficulty level, and treatment by the computer studies teacher. As in the previous chapter, the analysis focuses on *the process* of the students' attempts to exert influence, *the responses* of the teachers and head teacher, and *the results* of the negotiations. The communication and relations between students and adults and how they differ when the negotiations take place are of special interest here.

Background

The national Child and Recreation Programme mainly attracts young women from working class backgrounds with low cultural capital, often from homes with poorly-educated parents (Lidegran, Börjesson, Nordqvist and Broady, 2006), and the students themselves have some of the lowest marks from lower secondary school (Swedish National Agency for Education, 2008). This corresponds well with the background of most of the seventeen girls and four boys in the class studied here. Furthermore, some of their parents were on long-term sick leave or unemployed at the time of the study. Two of the students had an immigrant background.

The Child and Recreation Programme has generally had declining numbers of applicants in recent years and a large proportion of students with special needs (cf. Lemar, 2001). This was also the case at Ulmus School. School heads and student counsellors tend to recommend students who are uncertain of their choice or are otherwise difficult to place to attend this programme because of its supposedly caring and personality developing character. The head teacher at Ulmus School, for example, described the contents of the programme as 'A very good foundation to stand on as a human being'.

As seen in the previous chapter, education at Ulmus School in general was characterised by strong classification with, for example, distinct borders between academic and vocational programmes. In contrast, the Child and Recreation Programme was characterised by invisible pedagogy with weak classification and framing (Bernstein, 2000). It stood out because of this. The weak classification could be related to the fact that the previous child minder education was considered to have been too narrowly focused on childcare, and in the national programme, which was established in 1993, the ambition was to involve leisure time as well. The teachers had to create the programme specific character subjects themselves, as there was no tradition to provide guidance. As shown by Lemar (2001), this meant that none of the teachers had exactly the right qualifications for the character subjects, especially not for the part concerning leisure time. This general situation also applied to the teachers at Ulmus School.

As in Lemar's (2001) study several teachers of character subjects, and the head teacher, had backgrounds as preschool or child care teachers. Concepts such as *co-operation, personal relations* and *the student in focus* are, in contrast to the traditional subject knowledge in upper secondary school, characterising notions (in both the pedagogic practice and the teachers' professional identity) in the Child and Recreation Programme (Lemar, 2001). Like the working-class women taking health care courses observed by Skeggs (1997), the Child and Recreation teachers at Ulmus School talked about their duties as encompassing not only teaching the students about how to take care of people, but also caring for, and listening to, the students in a personal way. Skeggs argues that this coupling of profession, 'to take care', and personal relations, 'to care for', with the latter by tradition placed on par with female duties, constitutes these institutions as specifically female. Moreover, such caring responsibilities, which are closely connected to historically constituted female domestic duties (Ve, 1982), also contribute to the weak classification of the Child and Recreation Programme, with indistinct borders between the inside and outside of the institution (Bernstein, 2000).

The weak framing was, for example, expressed by teaching being mostly carried out with at most short briefings (sometimes none) with unclear guidelines from the teachers. The students often worked in small groups, which due to high absenteeism among the students often contributed to confusion and time-wasting for those who were at school. The students also frequently went in and out of the classroom, often without asking for permission, for example when fetching forgotten material from their lockers or going to the lavatory. When teachers tried to regulate the pacing by, for example, setting deadlines for tasks, the available time was always extended because so few had finished the task on time. Many students came to lessons late, and both extra breaks and reduced lesson times were very common. As in Lemar's (2001) study, the teachers often talked with the students about personal matters during lessons, and in the middle of subject teaching. Both teachers and students also often talked about ill-health. For example, students often complained about headache and pains in the stomach or back during lessons.

The programme has low status at upper secondary school, where the focus has traditionally been, and still is, on subject knowledge (Lemar, 2001). The low status was something the teachers, head teacher and students at Ulmus School were aware of and sometimes talked about with frustration. According to Bernstein (2000), there is space in categories—in this case programmes and character subjects—in which groups can develop their own internal rules and special voices. However, the crucial spaces that govern power relations in the school are those between the categories. Even if the focus on personal relations and caring for the Child and Recreation Programme students might be perceived as a factor that could increase the popularity of the programme, these characteristics did not seem to bestow high status in the school as a whole, especially in relation to programmes giving priority to academic skills and knowledge in traditional subjects. As in Lemars' (2001) study, this situation resulted in teachers sometimes feeling exploited, since although they were praised for taking care of students with special needs, they had low status in the upper secondary school system because of the caring orientation.

Formal and informal influence

Like those in the Natural Science class (see chapter four), the Child and Recreation students had little interest in joining the students' council at the school (cf. Danell, Klerfelt, Runevad and Trodden, 1999; Öhrn, 2004; Kamperin, 2005a). Most of the Child and Recreation students explained that they did not want to be the one who had to speak for the whole class at those meetings. However, two girls, Sofie and Jennie, agreed to be class representatives during the autumn term. The following term two others were supposed to take on this responsibility, but after the first term no one was willing to take over from the girls. As in the Natural Science class, there were only two class meetings during the field-year, and no one seemed to take these meetings seriously. Moreover, the general idea to raise current issues for discussion during the weekly class hours was generally not realised in this class. Instead, the class hours were primarily used to have a cup of coffee (organised by the students), and get information from the class teachers. In addition, towards the end of the spring term the head teacher started a 'CR-council' (Child and Recreation council) with two main purposes; to give her as the head an opportunity to regularly meet the students, and give the students opportunities to talk, and express opinions about their education without the teachers listening. There were two representatives from each of six Child and Recreation classes in this council at Ulmus School.

During lessons the students were often invited by the teachers to exercise influence informally in minor matters, for example modes of presentations, and the time for the next test. Öhrn (2004) and Kamperin (2005a) also commonly observed this kind of direct influence in the schools they visited, which may be regarded as a limited and individual way of influencing matters (Dovemark, 2004a). Moreover, the students took the initiative to negotiate about reducing lesson times and having extra breaks almost daily. Usually, it was one of three girls—Jennie, Iris and Sofie—who negotiated successfully with the teachers. Typically, one of them made a suggestion and the others gave support. Their arguments were often about having worked well for a supposedly long time (about fifteen to twenty minutes), and not being able to concentrate any more. Almost daily, the teachers listened to their suggestions, changed the plans, and the students got time off. The girls' agreements with the teachers often held for everyone in the class, including students who sometimes had a different opinion but did not talk about it openly. Those girls seemed to be aware of the importance of talking politely and preparing constructive arguments when they wanted the teachers to listen to their arguments (for a more detailed analysis of these aspects, see Hjelmér, Lappalainen and Rosvall, 2010). These have also been shown to be features of successful student approaches in previous studies (e.g. Öhrn, 2004; Kamperin, 2005a; Arnot, 2006). Using Giddens' (1984) definition of resources as capacities to change the material and social environment, one may therefore conclude that the girls had resources to influence classroom events and discourse in certain respects.

The teaching situation in computer studies

In computer studies the class was divided; half of the class was taught by a female teacher together with students from another class, and the rest of the students had a male teacher, here called Alf. I only visited lessons when the whole class was gathered and did not include other students, hence I did not participate in the computer lessons. However, I participated and talked with the students during lessons and breaks before and after the computer lessons, and I also raised this action during the interviews with students and head teacher.

Computer studies is a rather new subject in upper secondary school, and is not included at compulsory level. It is characterised by weak classification, as all teachers are expected to have some basic competence in handling computers, and all subjects and teaching rest on such skills. In other words, they are not monopolised by the subject of computer studies. Moreover, computer studies have only recently been included in teacher education, and only in some of the Swedish universities. In upper secondary schools, the staff teaching computer studies may or may not have teachers' training certificates, with or without formal ICT qualifications (Segerbrant, 2010).

Even from the beginning of the autumn term students from Alf's class expressed displeasure with the teaching, mainly because the difficulty level was too high, the pace too fast, and the teacher (who was said to lose his temper and disappear from lessons too often) gave insufficient help. The students described a teaching situation with almost no whole class briefings, unclear guidelines about what to do and high demands to take responsibility for their own studies.

> *Sofie:* We got almost no instructions about what to do, but more 'Now, you just have to do this' and so on.
> *Katarina:* And then, if you didn't understand he was unpleasant and didn't answer the questions you asked. (---)
> *Jennie:* Then you had to find the things you thought you should do.
> *Sofie:* Yes, and there were so many things that should have been done.

Jennie: You had to take a chance and guess what it was you were supposed to do.

Iris: Yes, and no one checked what we were doing, it was as if we only did like that and then we had the test. (Group interview, March 2009)

Although the situation with few briefings and unclear guidelines was not unique to this subject, the students were not used to facing such high demands in terms of autonomous work, high pace and difficulty level. Furthermore, they were not used to teachers who were angry and did not help them. On the contrary, most of the other teachers were very helpful and often used lesson time to talk and listen to the individual students. Some of the girls felt that girls, especially, did not get attention from the teacher.

It was like he totally forgot me and Anna during the whole lesson and acted as if we weren't there. He said he had some kind of impaired hearing that makes it hard to hear girls' voices because of their pitch. Er, perhaps it's not so good to be a CR [Child and Recreation Programme] teacher then, with a majority of girls in the classes?

(Malin, group interview, April 2009)

Very differently from what the students were used to, they were not allowed to take breaks during the lessons. Some of the girls found the situation in computer studies especially galling as the teacher himself often left the classroom.

Jennie: Yes, he walks out from the lessons all the time, and then when we...

Iris: Yes, he's away for five or ten minutes.

Jennie: Yes, and then when we have a seventy minute lesson, and say 'But can we have five minutes break?' 'No, no, you have to work' (Jennie imitates the teacher and makes her voice sound severe and angry).

(Group interview, March 2009)

The process of influencing

Initial silence

Although the students were displeased with the teaching situation in the computer lessons, they did not take the initiative to talk to either the teacher involved or the class teachers about the problems experienced, apart from the girls' attempts to negotiate extra breaks mentioned above. As in other situations observed during the field year only a few of the students, often the girls quoted above and their friends, negotiated with the teachers during lessons. In the interviews, many girls and all of the boys said they found it very hard to speak in front of the class, and kept quiet. The boys' and some girls' reasons for being silent included, for example, not bothering or coping any more, and thinking that speaking would not change anything anyway. However, many of them also talked about personal characteristics and feelings, such as not being the kind of person who likes to talk in front of people, uncertainty that their thoughts were good enough to share, and fear of shaming themselves in front of their classmates. Different framing principles from school give different experiences, which in turn determine what is possible to think and do (Bernstein (1990), implying that it is not individuals that have experiences but subjects that are constituted by the experience (Skeggs, 1997). In accordance with previous studies of working-class boys and girls, this indicates that these girls and boys from homes with low cultural capital experienced a lack of resources when trying to make teachers listen to them in school (Arnot and Reay, 2004; Arnot, 2006). The experience of not grasping the realisation rules governing pedagogic communication in school (Bernstein, 2000) may be one of the reasons why these girls and boys, from the beginning of upper secondary school, seemed to have deeply rooted perceptions of themselves as not being persons who speak aloud, or are worth listening to, in the classroom.

Even so, there were also some differences between the girls and boys with respect to bothering or not. When I asked the girls about things that could be influenced, they did in fact express opinions, for example, on easier textbooks, the content of sports days, examination forms, and free notebooks to help keep their notes in better order. Several girls also voiced disappointment with an education that so far had not been about what they expected. 'I applied for Child and Recreation because I wanted to learn about children', 'I thought it should be more about children and leisure', and 'It's really never anything about children and leisure time itself', they complained. It became apparent during the interviews that rather than not having opinions about their education, those girls considered school as a place where they could not be persons who influenced what happened.

> *Alice*: I just am, and I sit around for the day. I do what I should and then I go home as fast as possible. (---)
> *Carina*: Mm, so it doesn't feel that important for you, does it [to give your opinion during lessons]?
> *Alice*: Well, it's more that I haven't talked so much ever in my life.
> (Interview, March 2009)

In the extract above, Alice also seems to depict herself in line with the persistent assumptions that construct girls as dutiful school students who silently try to do what they believe they are expected to do (Gordon, Holland, Lahelma and Thomson, 2008). Historical circumstances may also have contributed to the girls having opinions about their education. In Sweden, traditionally female occupations (e.g. preschool teaching) have required studies in higher education more than traditionally male occupations (e.g. mechanics), for which upper secondary education is often sufficient (Arnesen, Lahelma and Öhrn, 2008). Still, even if these girls seem to think education is important and think of themselves as learners in school, it is with reservations. As in Johanssons' (2009) study of girls in the Health Care Programme, another female-dominated vocational programme, a majority of the girls in the class talked about themselves in a negative way, saying for instance 'I can't understand a thing', 'I will not have passed the test'. This is also in line with results in Skeggs' (1997) research, where the working-class females were busier with avoiding failures and losses than seeking ways to influence issues or processes in school.

In contrast to the girls, the silent boys seemed to have neither opinions nor knowledge about their education and the situation in school on the whole. Even when explicitly asked, Karl told me 'I don't have much to say about influence, and I don't want to decide about many things'. Other boys gave similar responses. Similarly to the working-class boys that Öhrn (1998) observed, they neither seemed to have acquired the legitimate pedagogic code like boys from homes with high cultural capital (e.g. the Natural Science class, chapter four), nor fought against the order in school like boys in groups Willis (1977) investigated. In contrast to those observed in Öhrn's (1998) study, the boys in this Child and

Recreation class did not bother about marks. Moreover, similar to the finding of Arnot and Reay (2004) that a majority of boys from working-class homes saw learning as something beyond, rather than within, their own control, the boys in this class seemed to believe that teaching and learning matters were the teachers' responsibility, not theirs. Yet, not bothering about their studies might also partly reflect a wish to appear cool, and distinctly different from boys who work hard at school, as frequently reported in educational research (e.g. Epstein, 1998; Francis, 1999; Frosh, Phoenix and Pattman, 2002; Jackson, 2006; Francis, Skelton and Read, 2010). The boys' approach may also represent a way of avoiding work and risks (Öhrn, 1998, 2002b).

Resources used by students

Research in compulsory schools indicates that the girls take responsibility to a greater extent than the boys and are driving forces when students try to influence things in school (Öhrn, 2004; Kamperin, 2005a). Previous research has also highlighted the importance of working-class girls' friendship when using networking as a possibility to act (Berggren, 2001), and for establishing positions of influence in schools (Gordon, Holland and Lahelma, 2000). These patterns also emerged in the negotiations in this class. Some of the girls talked to their closest classmates about the troubling situation in computer studies. 'You complain to a peer if something has been wrong', they told me.

Some of the girls, but none of the three boys, talked to their parents at home, and some of them asked their parents to act, when they found it uncomfortable to speak with the computer studies teacher themselves. After a situation when several students did not obey the teacher's repeated demands to close down MSN (a community on the internet), he became very angry at one of the girls, who felt offended. She talked to her father about what happened and asked him to act, then he phoned the head teacher. At the regular parents-teacher meeting, shortly afterwards, one of the parents talked about her daughters' complaints and other parents joined in. According to Marie, one of the class teachers, the parents had been seriously committed and 'Wanted the school to act'. She and her colleague were very surprised because the students had not talked to the class teachers or the computer teacher about the matter. The next day she informed the head teacher and, thus, the parents seemed to comprise a strong and effective resource for the students in this situation (cf. Öhrn, 2004).

Three days after the parents-teacher meeting, during one of Marie's lessons in a character subject, the head teacher and a head trainee came to see the class.

The head teacher stands in front of the class and says: 'I understand that you have opinions about one of your teachers'. She explains that Marie [one of the class teachers] has told her that the parents talked about it during the parents-teacher meeting last Monday. Now she wants to hear their version. None of the students say anything. After some seconds of silence, Marie says that it is about Alf who only teaches half of the class in computer studies, and that it is really important that they themselves tell the head teacher what it is all about. Some of the girls then say with very weak voices that they do not feel comfortable talking in front of the whole class about this matter. The head teacher continues: 'If you feel uncomfortable talking here in front of everybody, please come to my office and talk to me alone instead'. Iris then answers (with emphasis): 'He ignores what we're saying and doesn't listen at all'. Sofie continues by saying that he has mood swings, and he can get abruptly angry and sharp. Marie (turns to Irene): 'Irene, can't you describe how it is?' Marie also whispers something about Irene's mother talking a lot at the meeting. Irene sits quiet, and the head teacher again says that they can come to her office instead if they want to. Irene then answers with a weak voice: 'Everything has to go very fast, otherwise he gets irritated. It's hard to get it done in time'. Iris follows up, more distinctly, saying that it is really quite hard the things they are doing even if it is Word, but she says the teacher seems to think that they should already know this. 'He doesn't seem to understand that we think this is too difficult'.

None of the students say anything more now, and it is quiet in the class room. The head teacher has taken notes during the discussion. She then again encourages the students to come to her room and make sure they all know where her room is. Eskil [trainee head] asks if they think the greatest problem is that the teacher ignores them or that he moves forward too fast. Sofie answers distinctly: 'Yes but it's both, and then he's so often unpleasant'. Marie says to Linda: 'Linda, do you have Alf?' Linda answers with a very weak voice: 'Yes'. Marie then asks if she does not think there is a problem. Linda again answers very weakly: 'Yes'. The head teacher tells Marie that Linda does not want to talk in front of the whole class. She continues by saying that she will now talk to the computer teacher to hear his opinion. Perhaps he has not understood the importance of what they have said, and it is essential that he knows. After talking to the teacher, she will visit their next computer lesson. She concludes this discussion by again inviting the students to come to her office and talk, saying she will be glad if they do.

(Field notes, September 2008)

There is a strong emphasis on feelings in the discussion above, and the girls repeatedly talk about the teacher's mood swings and inability to understand their feelings in the problematic situation with excessive demands. Conversely, no one talks about the risk of failing to meet course goals or getting low marks if they cannot assimilate sufficient knowledge and skills through the mode of teaching. The girls negotiate from their experience, but, as in Skeggs' (1997) study, their lack of cultural capital reduces their possibilities to talk about studies in school (Bourdieu, 1994). Moreover, their arguments also seem to be in line with the pedagogic code of the vocational, female-dominated Child and Recreation Programme, which implies a focus on personal relations and feelings more than subject knowledge (Lemar, 2001).

Apart from Iris and Sofie, who belonged to the small group of girls that regularly negotiated and pursued issues in the classroom, only Irene talked during the meeting. These girls seemed to have relatively high competence and awareness of how to talk and negotiate with teachers. In the interview the girls underlined the importance of talking 'kindly but firmly', and in a constructive way 'Not just screaming ... more of a serious thing, to say why, our reasons for thinking this is necessary' (see also Öhrn, 1998; Kamperin, 2005a). Iris and Sofie also directly followed up and supported each other and Irene, as illustrated by the extract above (cf. Öhrn, 1998, 2005). On the whole, the need for support from friends when raising matters in the classroom was emphasised by several girls, and was usually met by discussing the matter with each other in and after school. In the example below, Jasmine explains how she needs to be sure there are at least two or three others who have the same opinion as herself before raising issues.

You dare to say what you want if you see, two, three persons who think almost the same, that's how it is ... Otherwise, if you don't know what the others think, oh then you'll have many thoughts, such as perhaps the others don't think like you...

(Jasmine, group interview, April 2009)

Even though there had been no joint discussions during breaks or lessons, all of the students told me a similar story about the conditions in computer studies. While all of the girls seemed to agree that the situation was not acceptable, the three boys in Alf's group gave the impression of not being bothered, even though they agreed with the description of the situation above.

> *Karl*: Yes, well, he was easily irritated when you didn't understand. (---)
> *Karl*: Well, I had no problems with it, it was just only some in the class who had.
> *Jonny* (chuckling): ... such as Laura.
> *Carina*: Okay, so that means you didn't experienced any major troubles then?
> *Karl*: No.
> *Jonny*: No, a little bit bad-tempered but...
>
> (Group interview, April 2009)

The boys, again, signal that they do not bother about such matters, even if others do. The reasons for them thinking like that could be that the teacher seemed to have treated girls and boys differently, for example, by not paying attention to the girls. Nevertheless, by giving the impression of not bothering the boys again avoided work and risks (see also Öhrn, 2002b). This, in turn, could mean that the agentic girls took responsibility for the situation in a traditional female way, which does not necessarily imply that they had a position of power (Walkerdine, 1990). However, the 'well-behaved' girls in this class, who were appreciated by the teachers for talking politely and presenting constructive arguments, were often an influential resource for the whole class in making the teachers and the head teacher listen to their arguments (see also Öhrn, 2005).

Responses from adults

Following the meeting with the parents, the class teachers did not discuss the situation with the students themselves, for example, during one of the class hours. Instead, the very next day the class teachers talked to the head teacher. Thus, from the outset they handed over responsibility for the situation to the head teacher, and seemed to have confidence in her ability to take action. Marie told me this was the natural way for her to proceed in a situation like this when the parents wanted the school to act. Moreover, the head teacher talked about acting quickly as her duty, both in relation to the students, especially as one of them felt offended, and the teacher concerned, who did not want to hear about the complaints months later. According to the head, her long experience of working as a head teacher was helpful when she planned how to act in this specific situation. This means, she saw it as important to talk to the students themselves, without the computer teacher first, to hear their version of events.

> *Carina*: You visited one lesson and talked to the students separately, and then the teacher separately, before you visited one of the lessons. How did you think when planning like that?
>
> *Headteacher*: I have also done the opposite on other occasions, but it usually ends up with wrangling and everyone defending themselves, especially the teacher defends himself/herself and accuses the students too often. Maybe it's only human to act like that, but it doesn't end up with a good result.   (Interview, May 2009)

Previous studies have shown the importance of support from teachers who are willing to listen when students want to exert influence (Öhrn, 2004; Kamperin, 2005b). Oscarsson (2005) argues that good relations between teachers and students are the basis for successfully fostering democracy in school. Such support was clearly visible in this case. At the meeting, the head teacher and class teacher listened, and encouraged the students to talk. The head teacher underlined the importance of students' opinions by inviting them to her office for discussions and by taking notes during the whole meeting.

Previous research has also shown the importance of not only helping but also supporting and educating the students to be politically aware, with knowledge of various strategies and options that could be applied (Öhrn, 2005). Similarly, Davies (1999) states that if students are to acquire any power and influence in schools they must have opportunities to practice actions, decision-making and responsibility-taking. In this Child and Recreation class the obliging head teacher took responsibility for the whole process, and the students were listened to, but not encouraged to take further part in the action.

It seems that the focus on personal relations and care about the students in this way led to the students being denied agency. Moreover, the adults' perceptions of these students as low-achieving and needy appear to have guided the way they chose to take care and act in the computer situation. In the extract below, this is illustrated by one of the teachers, when she underlines the need to support the students so they will become self-confident and employable when completing the programme:

> You [the teachers] have to repair what the compulsory school has destroyed; to take care of, to confirm, to listen to, to be empathic. And during these years make them [the students] feel they are good enough so that they can go out and work as a child minder.
>
> (Character subject teacher, group interview, May 2009)

As in the extract above, the teachers, as well as the students themselves, often seemed to have low expectations for the Child and Recreation students' achievements in school. Bernstein (2000) argues that the hierarchy of the school, with the academic student as the norm, has the unspoken power to show the sort of student the others should compare themselves with. This means that the Child and Recreation students will not only have low status in the eyes of others in school, but also in their own. They will always be compared, and compare themselves, with the 'academic student', who in a school like this is understood to be the 'normal student'. Similarly to the women in Skeggs' (1997) study, it is easier to say what kind of student the Child and Recreation student *is not* (e.g. not good at independently working in groups, not high-achieving in maths, not having a rich vocabulary) than what s/he is.

After the meeting with the students, the head teacher talked to the computer teacher and visited one of his lessons with the class. There seemed to be less hesitation about criticising a colleague's teaching in this situation than in the situation, discussed in chapter four, that developed in mathematics lessons in the Natural Science class. The weaker position of the teacher when teaching a short course in a new and weakly classified subject, was probably an important reason for this (Bernstein, 2000). Additionally, he had also diverged from the caring pedagogic code with its strong emphasis on personal relations in the Child and Recreation Programme, as he was perceived as ill-tempered, unhelpful, and demanding by the students.

Somewhat later, the head teacher checked with some of the students and heard that they were very pleased with how things had developed in computer studies. I asked Linda about the situation a month after the lesson with the head teacher, and she affirmed the head teacher's impression. While previously feeling uncomfortable with the computer lessons, she now almost looked forward to them, she told me. She appreciated that the computer teacher had promised to change in front of the whole class. Furthermore, she was pleased that the teacher was in a better mood and more helpful than earlier, and he had reduced the difficulty level and pace. After the head teacher was informed about the improvement, the action had come to an end. Thus, in these respects the class teachers, the head teacher and the parents had proved to be very effective resources for the students to draw on in their attempts to influence the situation in computer studies. However, the results were not entirely positive, as discussed below.

Results of the attempts to exert influence

Almost all of the students' claims resulted in changes: slower pace, lower difficulty level, more help from the teacher, and more balanced treatment from the teacher. Although the action seemed to be successful, a somewhat different picture emerged in the interviews with the students after the end of the course. Certainly, the students still thought the teacher had changed for the better but, as Karl says 'It was as though he became very sloppy and lazy instead' and Linda was not completely pleased any more.

> *Linda*: After that it was almost too lazy.
> *Carina*: Yes…
> *Linda*: I felt as if, in a way, since we engaged the head teacher because the pace was too fast, it was as if he made it too slow instead. So, while the other group that had Signild, or whatever her name was [the other computer teacher], they had done four computer things when we only managed three.   (Group interview, April 2009)

The missing 'computer thing' that Linda talks about was one assignment out of four in the course that was supposed to be used in a thematic project at the end of the year, involving several subjects. It seems that Linda and the other students, who were very pleased with the change directly after the head teacher's intervention, began to have doubts after the course. After a while they started to feel that the pace was too slow, and understood that they risked missing course contents. However, to raise critique against this appeared to be almost impossible in the class concerned. On the whole, students extremely rarely expressed disapproval about the risk of missing teaching contents openly. In the extract below, one of the few high-achieving girls describes how it felt impossible to display herself as an ambitious student in this context.

Anna: There was one situation when one of our teachers asked if we had brought a special paper with us, and nobody had, except me. Yet, I didn't put up my hand, and I can't understand why I didn't (laughs a little).
Carina: No.
Anna: I felt that it was like a reflex. Yes okay, nobody put up their hand, then I won't do it either.
Carina: You didn't want to attract attention?
Anna: No, so it's things like that, but you have to try to change yourself, dare to become tougher, you know.   (Group interview, April 2009)

Thus, the students seem to have difficulties in picturing themselves as high-achieving and ambitious in this context. Often, as in the extract above, the girls blame themselves for not being able to communicate in the classroom. Although Anna has no good explanation for acting as she did, she ends up blaming herself (Skeggs, 1997). 'Like a reflex', could be seen as an excellent analogy of what Bernstein describes as implicitly acquiring the pedagogic code of the school (Bernstein, 2000). She has difficulties in explaining this reflex but takes it for granted, as given by nature. This unspoken code, which works as a reflex, has the power to steer the students of this female-dominated vocational programme to communicate shortcomings about studies, instead of standing out as ambitious and high-achieving students.

Furthermore, neither the head teacher nor the class teachers followed-up the teaching and students' achievement on the course. In an evaluation by the Swedish National Agency for Education (2009b), it was concluded that successful compulsory schools managed to combine a caring and student-focused attitude with knowledge orientation. In this Child and Recreation class, it seems that care for the students was excessively prioritised. As was also evident from Lemar's study (2001), the diverse roles that the teachers involved in the Child and Recreation Programme had to play (e.g. social welfare officer, social worker, educator, mother, supervisor, knowledge intermediary) sometimes hindered attainment of the goals of the course.

The focus on personal relations seemed to cause work for these teachers even during breaks. 'Not many teacher offices have so many daily knocks at the door as ours, lots of students look for us, and it could be about so many different things'. The multiple roles of the teachers in this Child and Recreation class seemed to result in the teachers being overworked, with difficulties in focusing studies and reaching goals. It seems that the pedagogic code of the Child and

Recreation programme, with its strong emphasis on personal relations and catering for the emotional needs of low-achieving students, led to a slow pace and efforts to maintain a good mood, downplaying goal attainment and other forms of achievement.

In the same way, the quick and prompt intervention from the head teacher implied that the students were not empowered to take action themselves; the action was very short and ended almost directly after it started. But the students did learn that the head teacher was a powerful resource (Giddens, 1984) for them to use in problematic situations at school, something many of them talked about, and also used, in different situations. By taking sides with the students and demanding that the computer studies teacher make alterations, the head teacher endeavoured to alter the imbalance in power to the students' advantage.

Denvall (1999) states, that such involvement by the head is an important factor for the chances of students successfully exerting influence. But by only focusing on mood and reducing demands, the students' 'increased power' resulted in reduced course items, and not additional power over the way they learned in school. In other words, even if the power imbalance was shifted to the students' advantage, in practice it led to confirmation of their position as low-achieving students in school.

Concluding remarks

The caring discourse with its emphasis on personal relations and the emotional status of the Child and Recreation students seemed to be prominent but also treacherous for the teachers and students involved. The programme appeared to be an institution constituted by a caring rationality (Ve, 1982). There were demands on the teachers to embrace many different roles and to take care of diverse students' personal development, a working situation that often made it difficult for the teachers to set bounds for their own work, and resulted in both the programme and students having low status in the upper secondary school where the focus was traditionally on subject knowledge.

According to Walkerdine (1990), being held responsible for the development of each individual student is an 'impossible fiction', which leads to female teachers being trapped in a concept of nurturance. However, it seems that not only the teachers but also the students observed in this study ran risks of being captured in a 'caring trap'. From their experience of pedagogic practice stressing personal relations and catering for students' health and needs, the girls built their negotiations on feelings, rather than on high scholastic ambitions. The obliging teachers and head teacher responded in accordance with their expectations of these students as needy and low-achieving, implicitly compared with the 'normal' (i.e. academic) student.

This implies that the caring discourse in the Child and Recreation Programme is not neutral but divides the students depending on class and gender and needs to be scrutinised and problematised. Otherwise, the Child and Recreation students will not acquire the legitimate pedagogic code, but instead cement their lowly position in the classificatory system of the upper secondary school and (subsequently) wider society (Bernstein, 2000).

Without pre-empting the final conclusions in chapter nine, I want to highlight some factors distinguishing the programmes, and students, investigated at the same school. At Ulmus School, there seem to be unequal power relations not only between head teacher and teachers, teachers and students, but also between teachers, and between students, due to programme and subject. The strong classification of contents and teaching in mathematics, and their weak classifications in computer studies seem to have contributed to differences in the possibilities to influence and critique, irrespective of the arguments. Furthermore, in the influencing processes, even if there were differences, the students in both classes used resources of a similar kind, but with quite different results. Partly conflicting with indications in previous research, e.g. Öhrn (2005) and Arnot (2006), respectively, the parents from middle-class homes were not a strong resource and the working-class students seemed to be the ones who successfully influenced their education and learning. However, the analysis of who had influence over what clearly showed that neither of the classes had true influence over the nature of their learning. The Child and Recreation students only managed to reduce the items covered; the changes their actions induced did not make the education more suitable for their way of learning or previous knowledge in terms of attaining course goals.

It seems that teaching in the two programmes differed profoundly, not only with regard to the subject content, but also concerning the whole pedagogic orientation, since there was a strong focus on feelings, relations and reducing time and demands in the Child and Recreation Programme, and on hard work and high achievement in the Natural Science Programme. Add to this the difference in amounts of cultural capital in the two classes, and the gap increases even more (Bourdieu, 1994). The Natural Science students with high cultural capital generated more capital, while the Child and Recreation students were busy avoiding failures and losses (Skeggs, 1997). It seems as if these students' routes to future adulthood are already clearly staked out. Obviously, neither the teaching nor the results of the students' influencing processes, are neutral but are dependent on class and gender and, if not challenged, will contribute to increased gaps between students in these different programmes.

Chapter 6

Pedagogic practice and influence in a Social Science class

Per-Åke Rosvall

Introduction

This chapter is based on data that were ethnographically produced during one year's field work in a Social Science class in Apel upper secondary school. The material consists of research data from lessons, interviews with students, teachers and the head teacher as well as local and national policy texts. The empirical data include field notes from sixty-four lessons of varying length in six subjects and breaks, thirty individual interviews with students, twenty boys and ten girls, six individual interviews with teachers and one individual interview with the head teacher. The interviews were carried out during the second half of the fieldwork, in the spring term of 2009.

In order to analyse democratic education in school the terms *being* and *becoming* (see Gordon, Holland and Lahelma, 2000; Arnot, 2006) have been used in relation to how lessons were organised and how this organisation conceptualised the students either as young citizens in the present (i.e. lived democracy) or adult citizens to be (pedagogic content). Bernstein's (1990, 2000) concepts of visible and invisible pedagogy and classification and framing have also been used in order to analyse classroom interactions and content. These concepts concern the framing of pedagogical discourse (Bernstein, 2003, p. 36f); where framing is strong the transmitter strongly regulates and controls pedagogical communication processes and where framing is weak the control over communication resources is more equally distributed between transmitters and acquirers.

The themes discussed in this chapter are those that most frequently emerged in the material produced, concerning the notions of being and becoming. The interviews provided important guides for the choice of illustrative lessons, and interactions within lessons. More specifically, in the individual interviews with the students, two teachers were often mentioned as providing examples of different ways of organising lessons. These teachers' lessons therefore are used as examples in the chapter, representing (to varying degrees) those of several teachers who organised their lessons in similar ways.

The chapter starts with a short description of the school, before presenting the analysis of the pedagogic practice and factors obstructing influence in classroom activities. Comments by the students in the Social Science class indicate that their experience did not encompass the exercise of influence and the analysis shows that the pedagogic practice did not promote student influence, even though introductions by some teachers had strong framing and others had weak framing. Here, strong classification of 'correct' answers is regarded as a key issue, which will be problematised. Then implications of gender in the communicative practices, i.e. this dimension of the reproduction of social norms, will be discussed. The discussion then turns to the students' becoming, drawing particular attention to the teaching and learning of facts and development of competences in the Social Science class, and how the students were conceptualised as citizens through fact-based education. In the final part of the text some concluding interpretations on the pedagogic practice related to being and becoming a citizen are presented.

Apel School

The school researched is a large upper secondary school, by Swedish standards. At the time of the study it had 1,600 students and offered fourteen of the seventeen national programmes. It was well established and did not suffer extensively from competition from independent schools (see chapter two). According to the students, Apel school was weakly exposed to competition because there were no comparable schools in the region, and students did not want to travel far and/or could not afford a place to live close to equivalent independent schools, which were all some distance away.

Despite the lack of exposure to heavy competition from the independent sector the school had experienced serious financial cutbacks. The reduction in public spending on education has commonly affected Swedish schools in recent years and has been extensively reported (Hansson, 2009; Edlund, 2010). Due to these cutbacks there were restrictions on new employment and dismissal notices were delivered to some staff, particularly younger staff-members, during the year of fieldwork. This had consequences for the staff, whose average age was already quite high. The teachers were organised in teams, each team being responsible for teaching all of the subjects, ordering books, issuing invitations to give lectures, arranging special theme days and programme-specific visits (for example to work places of interest to the students for future employment).

Teachers and head teachers mentioned that there was a hierarchy among the teams as core subject teachers tried to orient themselves towards the academic programmes, thus the most experienced core subject teachers became most frequently attached to these programmes. In other words, it was difficult for vocational programmes to attract core subject teachers and if they did it was usually the less experienced ones. Both younger core subject teachers and the head teacher regarded this as a problem as it hampered the exchange of knowledge between teachers; the younger teachers were less able to learn from the experienced teachers and were not able to disperse their knowledge of the latest research acquired during their teacher education to the more experienced core subject teachers.

The head teacher said that they had tried to change this order a couple of years before the research began, but they had to abandon this attempted reform due to resistance from the experienced teachers. The experienced teachers were influential because they outnumbered younger teachers and thus, according to the younger teachers, it was difficult to implement new ideas. Experienced teachers were also more influential because they held more administrative positions. The reason given by core subject teachers for their preference to work on academic programmes was that academic programmes provide courses at a more advanced level in core subjects than the other programmes do. In addition, the lessons of the academic programmes were held in the main building, and teachers attached to those programmes had their office spaces there. Teachers who had office space elsewhere expressed frustration over this, as they felt that informal information and decisions rarely travelled effectively outside the main building.

The teacher team responsible for the Social Science Programme was no exception to the pattern of age and experience described above. The teachers all had at least twenty-years of teaching experience, and most of them had been at the school for all that time. Some had only a few years left before retirement. They had worked together for a long time and agreed about many educational issues. For example, common aims in Swedish schools, are to develop students' factual knowledge, skills, familiarity and understanding. In Swedish these are known as the four Fs: Fakta [Factual knowledge], Förtrogenhet [Skill], Förståelse [Understanding] och Färdighet [Familiarity, sometimes also translated as accumulated experience]. The teachers held factual knowledge to be the most important:

> One needs to learn facts before one learns anything else. One needs a platform to develop a skill.
>
> (Gunnar; teacher, field notes, November 2008)

> You need a decent amount of facts before you can understand how things are connected together and how to analyse them.
>
> (Bengt; teacher, field notes, October 2008)

In accordance with the above generalisations, teachers of the Social Science Programme more commonly gave lessons that were lecture-like, with the teacher lecturing while standing by the white board, than the younger subject teachers of the vocational programmes (see chapter seven). The statement by Gordon, Holland and Lahelma (2000, p. 76), that in their research they 'were struck by the familiarity [of the pedagogic practice], based on our own school days' could be equally applied to the practice in the Social Science Programme, which could be described as traditional and conservative.

The traditional pedagogic practice was somewhat unexpected, since contemporary policy texts emphasise individual freedom and self-governance (Båth, 2006; Sjöberg, 2009). In addition, analyses of pedagogic practice in compulsory school have found indications of shifts in education towards individual freedom and thematic work (Sundberg, 2003; Dovemark, 2004a; Nyroos, Rönnberg and Lundahl, 2004). In these respects, upper secondary school in Sweden has been little researched, but Johansson (2009) and the results from the present project indicate that education in academic programmes is more traditional and conservative than education in vocational programmes. However, there are always exceptions and variations within programmes, between subjects, within the same subject and between programmes (Beach, 1999, 2008a), even in practices of the same teacher (Beach, 1999).

The students

The students in the Social Science class were in year one of a three-year programme and were 16-17 years old. As shown in chapter two (and Broady and Börjesson, 2006) the students most likely to attend the Social Science Programme are girls, although there is a quite fair mixture of girls and boys, as well as students with immigrant backgrounds. However, the studied class consisted of eleven girls and twenty-one boys, and no one with an immigrant background. The students' socioeconomic backgrounds were diverse, ranging from working class with parents who had limited education to middle class with parents who had some academic education; such a range is typical for the national cohort of social science programme students in Sweden (Broady and Börjesson, 2006). Some students in the class were study-motivated and knew what they intended to do next: 'I am going to Lund University to read law in order to be a judge' or 'I am going to join the police.' But there were also some who appeared quite unmotivated: 'As a sixteen-year-old it is impossible to get a decent job today, but I would rather work if it was possible,' as one student said (cf. Lundahl, Erixon Arreman, Lundström and Rönnberg, 2010).

Being: the pedagogic practice and the possibility for influence

Being, in this context, relates to the *learner's space* in the classroom and her/ his possibility to act according to her/his own volition. Here, both teachers' invitations to influence and students' own actions are of interest. As shown below, the students did not seem to attempt to exert much influence, even in situations where one might expect that they should, e.g. when they did not feel that they had been given sufficient instructions to solve a task:

> I find one group in one of the common rooms above the library. I ask the group if I can observe how they work. Jonas says that I am more than welcome since they don't know how to solve the task: 'Maybe you can explain it to us.' I ask if they can explain how they understood the instructions. Peter and Jonas give their explanations and I say that I understood it as Peter explained.   (Field notes, October 2008)

Even though they had not understood the task they did not try to influence or interrupt the pedagogic practice. There were also occasions when they were invited to influence, but did not respond:

> 9:43 The teacher says that they now have two weeks in which they can do whatever they want and asks if anyone has any suggestions. No one says anything. Jens says that they could take the time off. (---)
> 9:46 When no one makes what the teacher seems to think of as a serious suggestion he gives some himself. I cannot catch the suggestions (two or

three) but they involve working on vocabulary, which most of the students in the front nod 'yes' to. The teacher then decides that they will work on vocabulary.   (Field notes, January 2009)

Invitations by teachers to students to influence lessons were rare, and it is interesting to analyse why the students did not respond to the few invitations given. To set the scene for the analysis this text will start with the students' experience of exercising influence.

The students' experience of exercising influence

In the interviews the students in the Social Science class were asked if they thought they could influence things like the content of lessons, themes under study, study pace and study environment, and from these questions discussions developed about their experiences of exercising influence in their class. Many of the students referred to formal influence in class councils and students' councils in compulsory school as ways to exert influence. In the beginning of the school year there was a scheduled time for class councils, but it was never used since it was scheduled two hours after the last lesson that particular day. The students who mentioned that the time was never used were asked if they wanted to use it. Most of them said no, because they thought that the students' council never worked in the compulsory school and they did not think that it would work now either.

> They ask you what you want. Then nothing happens. It is how it always has been. It was the way it was in compulsory school. It is how it is now.   (Ruben, interview, March 2009)

Since class councils were not used and students' councils were not attended by any of the students, the councils did not seem to have much impact on the students' influence and they are not further considered in this text.

Few students gave examples of occasions when they had been encouraged to influence anything, or had themselves taken the initiative to influence things in general in school, and even less so the content of lessons. This expression of a lack of impact also corresponded to patterns recorded in the field observations. Therefore, when students occasionally said that they thought that they had had some influence, they were asked to give examples. Unfortunately they were rarely able to comply with this request and few examples were forthcoming:

Per-Åke: Do you think that you have influence over the theme under study during lessons?

Linus: Yes, we have! Maybe not the content, but how. If we will read a lot, have lectures or if we will work on a report.

Per-Åke: Is it like that in all subjects?

Linus: No, not in all subjects. Not in Geography. He [the teacher] only works on things. And not in Social Science. She only gives lectures.

Per-Åke: But in the other subjects you can?

Linus: Yes, exactly.

Per-Åke: Do you have an example of when the teacher changed things due to your opinions?

Linus: No! Not that I can think of right now.

(Interview, February 2009)

Linus talked about students influencing lesson content, but it appeared that students were generally dubious that it was possible for them to influence either this or ways in which problems associated with informal relations between students were addressed. Tina, for example, talked about a social science lesson when the theme under study was bullying:

> She [the teacher] brought up bullying and stuff. If the teacher asks you, you try to put some effort in and discuss bullying. Then, you know, you try to find good solutions to solve the problems with bullying and stop it. And then she [the teacher] wants to hear [our solutions]. But what's the point of telling her when she can't do anything about it? Because, you know, she doesn't do anything if we discuss bullying. What's the point then? (Tina, interview, February 2009)

Although critical, Tina adheres to rules of hierarchy, i.e. that the transmitter has to learn to be a transmitter and an acquirer to be an acquirer, which in school becomes 'the condition for appropriate conduct in the pedagogic relation' (Bernstein, 1990, p. 65). This appears to hold for students of both the Social Science and Natural Science Programmes (see, for example, the Natural Science students' negotiations described in chapter four). However, it does not necessarily apply to students of other programmes with other pedagogic codes (see, for example, the discussion of the Child and Recreation students' negotiations described in chapter five).

Tina experienced that the teacher, as a transmitter, introduced a theme that was pointless given that she (the teacher) could not do anything about it. Nevertheless, according to the hierarchical rule Tina put effort in as an acquirer since the teacher asked her to, as a sign of loyalty to the pedagogic relation. However, Tina added another dimension to the hierarchical rules, showing that there are rules not only between the transmitters and acquirers, but also between acquirers, i.e. between students. She expressed that if you try to influence school procedures you may lose more than you gain:

> *Tina*: I think that the teachers could vary their lessons more.
> *Per-Åke*: Do you mean the way you work?
> Tina: Yes!
> *Per-Åke*: Is that something that you think that you want to bring up if you had a class council?
> *Tina*: I don't know. You know, er, there are some that want to do as little as possible and are satisfied with the teacher standing by the white board lecturing. They might be surly and I doubt the teachers will change.
> (Interview, February 2009).

This signals the importance of an individual attempt to exert influence being grounded within the group. Tina does not want to risk acting against her peers' wishes.

The most common comment from the students about influence was that it took time, and time was the most frequently expressed reason why they did not try to get involved in changing things that they considered to be problematic. Trying to exert influence seemed to be considered a waste of time. Some of the boys said that they wanted to spend as little time as possible in school to get time to practice sport. They wanted instructions about what to do so they could do it as quickly as possible and then practice their sport. Dovemark (2004b, p. 665) gives some similar examples.

The pedagogic practice

During interviews with the students in the Social Science class discussions around the pedagogic practice in terms of instruction, time-space relations and communicative practices in the classroom came up. Two teachers—the geography teacher, Gunnar, and the history teacher, Hans—were mentioned more often than others and used by the students to exemplify strongly contrasting pedagogic practices. They are examples of teachers who gave instructions and organised time and place with strong (Gunnar) or weak (Hans) framing. However, both had strong criteria for what was recognised as the subjects' knowledge. In the pedagogy with strong framing the students felt comfortable since the requested knowledge was visible. In the pedagogy with weak framing the students appeared insecure and, as we shall see, asked for stronger framing. This pattern has also been described in Beach (2000, 2008a) as particularly noticeable in relation to academic students in subject areas that they regard as important. The weaker framing of lessons gave the impression of providing opportunities to exert influence, but since the subject knowledge had strong criteria the students asked for a stronger rationalisation of the pedagogic practice.

Stina described Gunnar's pedagogy as being very focused, meaning that he had expectations regarding 'what you have learned and nothing outside that':

> *Per-Åke*: How would you describe a good lesson?
> *Stina*: The best one I think is, er, Gunnar. He is very good. He teaches in a fun way. He is one of those funny old blokes. Yes, I think he is the best.
> *Per-Åke*: So you think, er, what he does is funny?
> *Stina*: Yes, and even if he talks about things that he has done, it still has to do with the theme of the lesson.
> *Per-Åke*: Does he have good exams as well? Like tests and presentations?
> *Stina*: Yes, not too difficult questions and the tests are not too long. About what you have learned and nothing outside that.
>
> (Interview, March 2009)

The students who commented on Gunnar's and Hans' pedagogy were all more comfortable with Gunnar's stronger framing.

Gunnar used a teaching design with a strong time and space frame, which did not alter very much from lesson to lesson. There was a clear routine: start of lesson; introduction of the theme; students working through questions on work sheets and finding answers in their textbooks; whole class working through the answers; summing up and end of lesson. The students expressed during interviews that they felt very comfortable with this routine.

Hans, on the other hand, did not follow a clear routine. Where and when tasks were to be solved varied. The tasks were commonly written on the white board, and questions to address were often open, such as: 'What is the reason for this?'

or 'Why did this phenomenon occur?' However, although the questions were open, answers considered to be sufficient, as in the field note below, were often quite narrow, in other words, the evaluation of the weakly framed questions was quite strong:

> Hans then says that they should find information about today's theme. On Tuesday they shall present information about when, where, how and why instances related to today's theme occurred. The textbook should be the main source of information, but the students can also use computers and books in the library. The students start to work and most of them leave the classroom. I feel a little confused about what they are supposed to do. Hans walks up to me and says that he wants to see who works with whom and he wants the students to reflect upon why some things change and others do not. He also reveals that the answer to today's task is that some states have not been put under pressure due to geographical reasons.   (Field notes, September 2008)

Hans' use of weak framing allowed the students to work in the classroom, library, conference rooms and common rooms. This was particularly common at the beginning of the year, but changed later during the school year when most of the students failed an exam and Hans did not seem to think they were taking enough responsibility. He said: 'You only go and put your books in the locker.' (Field notes, February 2009). After this, the students' worked in the classroom, as a way of keeping them under supervision and under control.

Instruction: time-space, control-autonomy

What was recognised as valuable content was clear in Gunnar's visible pedagogy, as expressed by Stina in the above excerpt. However, the valuable content in Hans' pedagogic practice was less obvious to the students, and they appeared uncertain about how to act during his teaching. Invitations to the students to explain their understanding of how to solve a problem were rare, from both Gunnar and Hans, and when they came the students' suggestions were seldom acknowledged by the teacher. The occasions observed all ended with suggestions by Hans or Gunnar, which the student could choose between.

Even when tasks were introduced with open questions, as in the practice of Hans, when examined verbally or in tests the requested knowledge was narrow and specific. It was observed that sometimes some of the students tried to give their understanding of how a task should be tackled, or a question addressed, but in the end Hans gave his explanation. In both Hans' and Gunnar's teaching valuable content was therefore of the same kind, i.e. data/facts, and in Bernstein's terms a visible pedagogy was apparent, characterised by a social relation of superiority from teacher down to learner.

The aspect that seemed to make the students uncomfortable with Hans' pedagogy, but not Gunnar's, was the lack of explicit and specific criteria. As Anna and Peter put it:

> I cannot say that I am very fond of Hans' pedagogy. He makes you feel indescribably stupid. It makes you say nothing, because if you do, you sort of get declared stupid. (Anna, interview, February 2009)

> Hans is the teacher who really wants us to speak, but in his lessons we are the quietest. (Peter, interview, March 2009)

Gunnar's pedagogy could have been described by the students as controlling, of a kind that precluded autonomy to explore tasks from their own perspectives and experiences. However, the students listed other dimensions as valuable that had to do with being explicit and specific. In contrast, Hans' pedagogy could have been recognised and valorised by students as giving them autonomy to explore tasks from their own perspectives and experiences, but it was not. The 'correct' answer seemed to be important. When there were contradictions between weak framing of instructions and strong classifications of correct answers, the students seemed confused and they asked for stronger framing of instructions. When the teacher narrowly defined the 'correct' answers it did not support the students' own reflections and explanations in a way that would recognise the students as active citizens. Strong classification means that few opinions and perspectives are relevant; weak framing of instruction disguises this relationship and confuses the pedagogic communication.

What was regarded as the 'correct' answer and what was evaluated were important aspects in terms of the kind of pedagogic practice the student asked for. Evaluation is here regarded broadly as teachers' responses to students' answers in both public interactions and tests. In this respect, neither Gunnar's nor Hans' pedagogic practice promoted influence because of their strong classification of what was evaluated. Hence, the students worked according to rationality, and searched for ways to identify what was evaluated, which in the practice of Gunnar and Hans did not encompass raising questions by oneself. When the primary objective for students is to find and reproduce answers to other's questions, they are classified according to categories over which they have little control, in a manner contrary to exercising influence and participation. Students become dependent and objectified rather than influential and active (cf. Beach and Dovemark, 2007, p. 54).

Most teachers of the social science class practiced pedagogy like Gunnar, that is, in the classroom and lecture-like, but not in such a time- and space-controlled manner.

Gender relations

Public interactions can be seen as opportunities for students to live democracy and to influence the present. However, as shown above, students in these examples did not exert much influence. All the teachers of the class except one, who had a structured way to distribute questions equally among the students, limited public interaction to a group of visibly active students, while the rest participated silently in interactions. Hence, an almost constant group of students were silent during almost all lessons:

> Lesson starts. After Gunnar has let all the students into the classroom he walks up the aisle. He starts to talk about the economic crises. Leaning forward and moving his hands, he asks question about the crises and the students answer. Boys answer, more boys answer, no girls. Gunnar talks quickly and throws questions to the students who are closest to him. No students further away get any questions. Gunnar talks back and forth and then comes to today's theme under study. (---)
> 10:38 The students start to work with work sheets. (---)
> 10:59 Gunnar calls the students' attention. He starts to work through the work sheet, top down. Gunnar reads the questions on the work sheet and lets a student answer. Sometimes by pointing to a student, sometimes a student shouts the answer without getting the question. Only boys close to Gunnar answer.   (Field notes, November 2008)

The framing of the public interaction was strong and led by Gunnar. He distributed questions to boys close by. It was unusual for girls to be heard in the public interaction. This somewhat conflicts with contemporary gender research showing girls to be more active in class than previously assumed (see, for example, Falk 1999, p. 136), at least in some lessons or subjects (Öhrn, 2000, 2002; Tallberg Broman, Rubinstein Reich and Hägerström 2002, p. 116). In this class, there was a large silent group, in which girls were over represented. None of the teachers tried, as far as I could see, to change this feature of public interaction. The students who were silent at the beginning of the school year were silent at the end. There was also quite a large number of boys who were quiet, but in the main it was girls that were silent.

> The boys are more involved than the girls. I don't know, but I think that all the boys, that they hog things a bit more than the girls. (---) It is how it is and how it always has been.   (Stina, interview, March 2009)

Most teachers largely relied on lectures and public questioning/discussion as a basis for their teaching. That only a few boys were active in the public interaction was noticed by the students and brought up during interviews:

> *Per-Åke*: Do you think that you are equally active in the classroom, as in raising hands, answering questions or in contact with the teacher?
> *Jens*: No, I suppose we are not! I know in Hans' lessons, in the beginning, no one raised a hand if he asked something, but everyone just sat quiet. The girls never say anything still, er, in any lesson.
> (Interview, March 2009)

Most of the students that raised this issue thought that it was the individuals' own responsibility to change '…and there are those who never talk. They have to blame themselves I suppose.' (Ola, interview, February 2009). But on individual students' possibilities to change the pedagogic code Bernstein (1990, p. 139) is very specific: 'If the pupils are to challenge the code effectively, it cannot be done by one pupil.'

I deliberately did not ask 'are girls and boys equally active' (see above excerpt). Nevertheless, most of the answers contained gender dimensions. Here, rather traditional gender regimes were observed, which might be explained by the somewhat conservative and traditional pedagogic practice and the observation that teachers seldom distributed questions equally among the students (which has been seen to correlate with more equal participation, see Öhrn, 1990).

> Yes, I think it is quite negative for the girls, that they are not heard. Often they know their answers are as good as the boys'. But since they are not heard during lessons it can make teachers believe that they [girls] do not know.   (Josefin, interview, February 2009)

Another contributory factor may have been that the kinds of conditions that promote girls' voices—such as: regular opportunities for communicating with teachers; a history of friendship and frequent meetings outside school; and small group activities when working with content in school (Öhrn, 1998)—were rarely, if ever, observed in this research.

Educational practices in which students were invited to exercise more influence were known at the school, and applied by younger teachers on other programmes, according to teacher interviews. Strong insulation between teacher groups working on different programmes and the hierarchy among them seemed to be major reasons why teachers of the Social Science Programme could hold on to their somewhat traditional and conservative pedagogic practise. It is important to note that the participation in public interaction did not affect influence concerning the pedagogic practice much, but rather it said something about how power relations were reproduced, since:

> ... rules, practices, and agencies [regulate] the legitimate creation, distribution, reproduction, and change of consciousness by principles of communication through which a given distribution of power and dominant cultural categories are legitimated and reproduced.
> (Bernstein, 2003, p. 113)

In other words, it might add to the reproduction of influence and silence; who speaks and who is silent. This relates to the learning of how to negotiate gender, to develop certain gender identities and how to 'do gender' (Connell, 2002). In relation to this the pedagogic practice in the researched class risked the reproduction, within the classroom as a local context, of a gender regime of male hegemony that does not contest existing gender order (Connell, 2002).

Becoming

The content in the education of the Social Science class has been analysed in order to illuminate questions of becoming. In relation to the concept of *becoming* (Gordon et al., 2000, p. 21) both classification and framing are relevant;

classification through the negotiations of categories and framing through selection of content (Bernstein, 1990, p. 37). The becoming section is shorter than the being section in this text since issues of being were more poignant. In this respect, there were differences between various classes. For example, in relation to becoming, the students in the Social Science class did not ask for more knowledge of a certain subject as preparation for a future vocation, unlike the students in the Vehicle class (see next chapter).

With a focus on facts

The national curriculum for the Swedish upper secondary school (Lpf 94) draws attention to the teaching and learning of facts and development of competences.

> Knowledge is a complex concept which can be expressed in a variety of forms—as facts, understanding, skills and accumulated experience—all of which presuppose and interact with each other. Education should not emphasise one aspect of knowledge at the cost of another. (---) Pupils shall have the opportunity of reflecting over their experiences and applying their knowledge.
>
> (Ministry of Education and Research, 1994, p. 7)

The observations from the researched class showed that there was a focus on facts. This will be further explored in relation to the students as becoming citizens.

At the beginning of the school year the students were not familiar with each other, since most of them came from different compulsory schools or classes, and initially most of the students were silent when asked questions by the teachers, and when teachers asked about their opinions about what to study. Teachers then decided the themes, often according to the themes in textbooks used in the subject. Some teachers let the students look at their textbooks before deciding, but there were never any suggestions from the students. The textbooks' impact on themes under study and the sequence varied in different subjects. In maths, the sequence of themes in the textbook was not questioned, while in social science they jumped back and forth between chapters, in accordance with the teacher's choice. In both social science and Swedish language, the teachers spent relatively little time following the textbook, and more often worked with information from the Internet or copied material. During the year this class was observed there was no thematic work in which teachers of different subjects worked together, which might have resulted in more crossing of subject boundaries.

The national curriculum for upper secondary education (Lpf 94) emphasises both transmission of facts and development of competences. If these aspects are typified as distinct pedagogic practices we can elaborate two different sets of instruction and evaluation forms, where fact-oriented education focuses on the transmitter; and competence-oriented education focuses on the acquirer. The foci of the pedagogic practices is visible through evaluation forms, since students' performance can be easily graded using simple criteria if the focus is on facts, while evaluation of more complex aspects of knowledge, such as understanding and skill, is required if the focus is on competence.

In the earlier examples of Gunnar and Hans we can see strong framing of what counts as legitimate knowledge and evaluation of performances that can be graded, with a strong criterion of knowledge that is visible through it being 'what you have learned, nothing outside that' and Hans' narrow definitions of what can be regarded as the right answers. These evaluation criteria regulate the distribution of power and construct a consciousness of what is thinkable or unthinkable (Bernstein, 1990).

This raises the question of what kind of citizens the students are educated to become. The curriculum describes a society that changes and emphasises schools allowing students to develop abilities such as taking an initiative and obtaining a democratic education that prepares them for the adjustments that will be required when conditions in working life and society change (Ministry of Education and Research, 1994, p. 8). Using examples from her ethnographic research, Borgnakke (2004) showed that learning by doing (that is, formulating problem questions for oneself) is essential for students to learn to be learners by themselves and to create knowledge from their own platforms by addressing questions raised by themselves. An example of this emerged when the students in social science worked on EU parliamentarianism. They were working in groups and I had the possibility to walk around and ask questions. Some of the students expressed frustration over the content they were working with:

> *Anna*: It is always about how to vote. Not about questions that really matter.
> *Tina*: Yes, what's the point of knowing how to vote when you do not know what you are voting about?   (Field notes, November 2008)

These students do not seem to be content with the focus on *forms* of formal influence and decision-making. Tina asks for knowledge about the targets or content of voting procedures, but judging from the fieldwork such issues were seldom addressed in class. The above example of the EU parliament also concerns distant processes, in the sense that the students, as sixteen year-olds, could not participate in the kind of formal democratic processes taught. However, here as in other instances discussed in this chapter, students did not act to change the content of the lessons, and a question that arose was if the students were satisfied with the influence they had on themes under study. The most common response, from the students was that it 'doesn't matter' or 'I don't bother':

> *Per-Åke*: Do you think you can influence content in lessons?
> *Robin*: Oh, it doesn't matter. The teacher is supposed to know, isn't he.
> (Interview, April 2009).

> *Per-Åke*: When and how do you think that you can influence things in school?
> *Saga*: The teachers asked us in the beginning what we wanted. But it was only then, not so much anymore. It's okay, er, I think.
> (Interview, March 2009).

> *Per-Åke*: How do you think that formal influence works in school?
> *Peter*: I have always been in a school where you have no power. So it doesn't bother me that much. But it would be better if one could be involved in how it should be done. (Interview, March 2009)

As shown above, during interviews the students in the Social Science class expressed beliefs that they did not have much influence over the themes under study. Robin and Saga feel that 'it doesn't matter' and 'it's okay' as it is. Peter, on the other hand, claims that it would be better if the students were involved. He says he wants to influence things now, but his words imply that he feels it would be futile to try to change the school's practices. There appears to be a reciprocal understanding between the school as an institution and the student. The 'pedagogic device' works as a symbolic ruler of consciousness in its positioning of pedagogic subjects (Bernstein, 1990, p. 189).

Here I want to refer back to the interview excerpts under the heading 'The students' experience of exercising influence: Being'. Some students indicated that the school did not 'feel real' and saw school as a means of transport to what they expressed as 'real life' or adulthood. They added that since school was not 'real' there was no point in trying to influence it. It would not have any real impact on their lives and it was not their problem, it was a problem for those who worked in school:

> *Per-Åke:* If there is a problem in school? What do you do to change it?
> *Robin:* Er, okay, I don't think that we put much effort into it you know. I think it's the ones that work here that have to deal with it.
>
> (Interview, March 2009)

Robin's answer gives the impression that he is not involved. School problems are for those who work there to solve.

Being and becoming compared

The students wanted strong framing and visible pedagogy, but according to previous research this does not promote student influence, as it treats students as raw material that has to be formed rather than as co-workers (Forsberg, 2000). Active student education and pedagogy focuses on students' experiences in relation to the subjects learnt (Lundström, 1999) and gives more possibilities for them to exert influence than education based on lectures (Borgnakke, 2004), and education with a strong emphasis on subject textbooks does not help students exercise influence since textbooks seldom presuppose student experience, but rather follow the logical order of a subject or discipline (Selander, 2003). In other words, what the students wanted does not promote influence according to previous research. Rather, it appears from the analysis to reflect a rational understanding of how to pass a course.

Influence over pedagogic practice is crucial in terms of being a citizen sufficiently to be given influence. It concerns the feeling of not only receiving but also giving something. However, it seems as if the term alienation could be applied in the cases considered here, and in a twofold way. First, to explain issues that concerned the students' feelings towards school, as manifested in their utterances about why they did not participate: 'What's the point?', 'It's the ones that work here that have to deal with it' (Robin), 'I doubt the teachers will change' (Tina). In addition, those utterances signal a possible use of the term alienation in a Marxist sense, of the students having no control over their working conditions and the products of their work. They 'play the game of school', but are not genuinely active in education as a collaborative project between transmitters and acquirers.

Beach (2008a), who has investigated the features and distinctions of visible and invisible pedagogy, proposes that efforts should be made to integrate and harmonise them, thereby 'emphasising and rewarding genuine *activity, collaboration and critique*, rather than a passive absorption and accumulation of knowledge' (p. 157, italics in original). If we examine the student interviews in the present research in terms of feeling involved, Beach's analysis also seems to be valid in relation to this material. Analysis of the students' experience of not being involved is important, because students who have opportunities to actively participate in the pedagogic relation (Hoskins, d'Hombres and Campbell, 2008) may be better prepared to have access to a discourse of their own becoming than those who are passive, who will, according to Bernstein (1990), be more dependent on the transmitter (teacher).

Collectively, weak influence over time and space, controlled communicative practices, and a pedagogic focus on facts go along in this class with students not feeling involved. They expressed feelings of 'what's the point', 'why bother' and were conceptualised towards a citizen that might be involved later. In relation to the pedagogic practice in the social science class this raises questions about their becoming. The curriculum text stipulates that students:

> ... shall receive a foundation for lifelong learning that prepares them for the adjustments that will be required when conditions in working life and society change. (Ministry of Education and Research, 1994, p. 8)

An education that focuses on facts, with a hierarchical structure, in which the teacher acts as bearer of the knowledge to be acquired, trains students to value information for themselves to a lesser extent. Content chosen by students, e.g. the ideologies of parties rather than decision routes within the EU, promotes knowledge in a vertical discourse and the valuation of information by the students themselves, that could be used for their development and influence.

In the public interactions most students were silent, or at least silent most of the time, while a small group of boys participated in the interaction with the teacher. It is difficult to say why the small group of boys broke the public silence, but of the five most active boys three were close friends from the same class in compulsory school. Peer relations therefore appear to be important (corroborating information presented in chapters four and five) as in previous research showing such relations to be important for girls' classroom actions and influence (Mac an Ghaill, 1998; Öhrn, 1998; Gordon et al., 2000; Berggren, 2001). However, in this class it was boys, not girls who seemed to benefit from such relations.

The gendered structure of public interaction does not, as Ohlsson (1995) noted, only have implications for issues regarding influence, but also for matters regarding learning outcomes. Through participating in public interaction, knowledge and language skills are developed (Ohlsson, 1995). In the class observed here only a small group of boys were consistently heard in public interaction (see also Lundgren, 2000). So, rather than asking questions about gender differences we might ask why a small group of boys broke the silence (although we still have to acknowledge that they were boys, not girls). It is also notable that participation in public interaction did not give explicit influence in the present practice, but reproduced power relations in terms who were voiced, which could be assumed to affect who will be voiced and have influence in the future.

Pedagogic practice, as exemplified by the practices of Gunnar and Hans, realised little of the curriculum goal of ensuring that 'all pupils actively exercise influence over their education' (Ministry of Education and Research, 1994, p. 14). Strong framing of facts as a learning outcome appears to be one explanation for this. Hans used—at the beginning of the school year—pedagogy with weaker framing, but since the outcome of results implies strong framing and classification with examination of facts students asked for explicit and specific instructions, i.e. visible pedagogy. Thus, paradoxically, Hans and the students 'returned' to what might be called a more traditional and conservative pedagogic practice (cf. Beach, 2008b), as a practice that was safe rather than dangerous (Bernstein, 2003, p. 76). The students need to know they will not fail exams and with the teacher as holder of the knowledge asked for, students prefer strong framing since it gives better opportunities for them to achieve well, even though it limits their possibilities of exercising influence. Thus, contradictions between the curriculum and what was seen in the pedagogic practice seem to derive from a search for consensus. This correlates with findings of earlier research in comprehensive schools (Nyroos et al. 2004, p. 754f), where pupils believed that they were 'not able to handle a high degree of freedom without goals and tasks, which help them reach the objectives.'

In this chapter it has been stressed that weak framing of instructions alone is not sufficient to promote student influence if classification of what constitutes the right answer is still strong. In this chapter material has also been presented about public interaction with traditional gender regimes that somewhat contradicts contemporary research. Finally, the pedagogic content oriented towards students learning to be adult citizens and about parliamentary forms, seems to conflict with the students' apparent interest in learning about ideology.

Chapter 7

Pedagogic practice and influence in a Vehicle Programme class

Per-Åke Rosvall

Introduction

The empirical data analysed in this chapter were ethnographically produced during one year's fieldwork in a Vehicle Programme at Apel upper secondary school. The empirical data consist of field notes from seventy-two lessons of varying length in six subjects and breaks, thirteen individual interviews with the students, all boys, five individual interviews with teachers and one individual interview with the head teacher. The interviews were carried out during the spring term.

The analysis of the interviews indicates that the boys in the class wanted more out of their education, for example in terms of core subject knowledge, lesson time, classroom order and access to student support. However, although all the boys said they wanted to be better educated in the core subjects, few acted to exert influence to get more teaching, broader educational material or a calmer teaching environment. In an attempt to understand these contradictions, I have applied Bernstein's concepts of horizontal and vertical discourse (Bernstein, 2000, p. 155) in the analysis. Horizontal discourse is defined by Bernstein as common-sense knowledge, which in practice is segmented and particularised. Vertical discourse, in contrast, is theoretical, abstract, esoteric and hierarchically organised. The latter encompasses competences and principles the boys asked for. The contradiction between the boys' expressed wishes and their lived practice is analysed and discussed in this chapter in relation to influence.

Influence can be analysed from diverse perspectives. In this chapter I have tried to present a wide range of the most pertinent examples from both character and core subjects. As in chapter six, the concepts being and becoming have been used to organise the material, but since the central themes that emerged differed between the two contexts, the examples presented in the chapter, and how they are presented and discussed differ accordingly.

The main aim in this chapter is to demonstrate the obstacles observed in the pedagogic practice that prevented the boys from influencing their education as they desired. This theme is developed under the heading Being. Factors addressed related to influence that affected the boys' being include the physical location of their education, peer relationships, constructions of masculinity and education about influence. In addition, I consider ways in which the pedagogic practice was affected by how they saw themselves as students and how teachers saw them as students (manifested in the distinction between what was seen as manual and what was seen as mental). Then, under the heading Becoming the educational content is examined in relation to the boys' possibility to exercise influence in their future, post-school work and adult life.'

Apel School

Many of the school activities were located in the main building. Most of the teachers, all head teachers, student support staff, student health care facilities, the building manager's office, dining hall, main cafeteria, assembly room, and most classrooms were located there. Students attending academic programmes such as the Natural Science and Social Science Programmes (analysed in chapters four and six, respectively) also had all their lessons there. However, some programmes with requirements for large rooms or areas, such as art/dance, construction, hotel and catering, and the Vehicle Programme, were based in dedicated buildings, most of which were close to the main building, but some were hosted for financial reasons in various places some distance away in old industrial constructions.

The Vehicle Programme was based in a building, in an industrial area, five hundred metres away from the main building, that housed three classrooms, a small cafeteria with a coin-operated coffee machine, a staff room for the teachers of vehicle-related subjects, an area for playing table tennis and three vehicle halls with garage equipment and space for working on vehicles. In this respect it was very different from the main building, which lacked rooms where students and staff could gather and engage in activities as a class. As it was a smaller class, wearing working clothes and adapting to a workplace timetable with morning coffee (instead of a school schedule with no informal gatherings during coffee breaks) provided foundations for a group identity and contributed to stronger connections between members of the class than was seen in the academic class analysed in chapter six. In addition, the organisation and use of these spaces had obvious resemblances to professional garages.

The Students

The boys in the researched class were in year one of a three-year programme and were 16-17 years old. The class, which consisted of sixteen boys, shared a vehicle hall with another class; one class spent the first half of each school week (Mondays, Tuesdays and Wednesdays until lunch) in the vehicle hall, then had lessons in core subjects (English, Swedish language, maths and physical education) on Wednesday afternoons, Thursdays and Fridays. The school year was divided into three periods. For two of the three periods all lessons were in the classrooms in the vehicle hall building, except physical education which was located in the school's sports hall. In one period they also had English and maths in the main building.

There was very strong gender homogeneity in both staff and students associated with the programme. All the teachers of its character subjects were male, and only one teacher of the core subjects was female. All the students in the class were male, with a working class background. Their parents had typical working class jobs, such as industrial labourer, cleaner, electrician or elevator repairer. Some of them had one or two parents who had retired early or were on long-term sick-leave.

Almost all students that applied to the Vehicle Programme at this school were accepted (and the vehicle students sometimes referred to themselves as low-status students, although they were proud of working with vehicles). The entrance requirements for the programme were low. About half of the class had experience of remedial teaching from compulsory school. Four of the boys had scraped passes in the core subjects, thus meeting the criterion for admittance to a national programme at upper secondary school. According to the boys there were schools where the Vehicle Programme has higher status, and at some—especially those with a special orientation, e.g. snow vehicles or aircraft, or schools close to vehicle manufacturing plants—the entry requirements can be quite high.

Being: to be a Vehicle student and possibilities to exercise influence

Being, in a student's educational context, relates to his/her space in the classroom and her/his possibility to act according to her/his own volition. Here, both teachers' invitations to exercise influence and students' own actions intended to influence the pedagogic practice are of interest (see chapter 6). As shown below, during the interviews the boys said that they wanted more education in core subjects and a calmer working environment during lessons, but during the fieldwork they seldom acted to induce changes in pedagogic practice, except to reduce lesson times (Hjelmér, Lappalainen and Rosvall, 2010). As shown below, peer relations and constructions of masculinity operated against actions of change. Their school identities can therefore be seen as encompassing conflicts between their identity within official pedagogic practice, and their constructed identity as 'real men'.

Being a Vehicle Programme student

Most of the Vehicle Programme students (hereafter vehicle students) were very proud of being vehicle students and of what they did in the programme. They put effort into doing things well and solving tasks in an appropriate manner. It was not unusual to hear both their teachers and the students themselves express, with apparent pride, that they were handy men rather than thinkers when at work.

According to Bernstein (2000, p. 55) 'identities are constructed by procedures of interjection' and 'regions are recontextualisations of singulars and face inwards towards singulars and outwards towards external fields of practice'. In other words, constructions of the students or themselves as manually rather than mentally oriented might exclude possibilities for mental work in the external fields of practice. Both students and teachers point to the boys' preference for manual work:

> Vehicle lesson [at the beginning of the school year]: The teacher goes to another room to get something. Niklas is leaning over the bench. I ask him if he is tired. He answers that he is not: 'It is sitting still you know. When you sit and listen to the teacher. I would rather do something. But I suppose you have to do this before you can do work with the customer's cars'. (Field notes, September 2008)

> Swedish lesson: Lesson ends. I wait for the boys to walk out before I go out myself. When I am about to walk out the teacher comes up behind me and says: 'You can really see that they don't like to be in a classroom.' (Field notes, October 2008)

In academic tasks too, teachers constructed the students as manual rather than mental. The following teacher, for example, used practical tasks as rewards for doing theoretical tasks:

> Vehicle lesson: It is starting to be bit noisy in the classroom. The boys are spending more time talking to each other than doing their tasks in the book. Teacher: 'The earlier you finish the chapters in your books, the sooner we can start to work with customers' cars.'
>
> (Field notes, January 2009)

Many of the field notes refer to what can be understood as students preferring to do things with their hands rather than tasks associated with books. Manual work was also connected to physical space, and sometimes to how they perceived themselves: 'I am better at things in the vehicle hall'. What they can imagine themselves doing is thus linked with physical space.

There was, of course, not only one kind of boy on the Vehicle Programme. For instance, the diversity in the boys' study backgrounds was reflected in how they acted during lessons. In the subjects Swedish, English and maths, which most of the boys regarded as theoretical or bookish, there were quite pronounced differences between the students who said that they had problems with the subjects in compulsory school and those who said that they coped with them, in terms of activity at lessons, leaving early if possible and attendance rate. Overall, there were also higher degrees of attendance and activity in lessons at the beginning of the school year. The students who indicated that they had experienced problems with the core subjects in compulsory school were those who gradually became less active. This had implications for their studies, as the students' own activity in seeking teacher attention was crucial in order to get help.

There were examples in all subjects of students who expressed that they had problems with learning in compulsory school being increasingly neglected by teachers. Three of those students switched to the Individual Programme or changed class. Thus, students who were not able to consume teacher time were eventually more likely to drop out.

When students can choose, to a larger extent, the time and place for their work it can be said, in Bernstein's terms, to have weaker framing. Beach and Dovemark (2009, p. 695) have noted that in a pedagogic practice characterised by weak framing and personalised learning students who did not consume teacher time fell behind and were said to be irresponsible and failing to make the right choices by teachers. In other words, upper secondary education in the Vehicle Programme did not compensate for missing knowledge from compulsory school or 'administrate a recovery plan' (Bernstein, 1990, p. 74).

The above examples, showing how the boys are constructed as manual rather than mental, were extracted from group activities and public classroom teaching. When the boys were interviewed, individually or in small groups, a quite different picture emerged. Both boys considered by teachers as low achieving and higher achieving talked about wanting to improve their achievements in the theoretical subjects, such as Swedish, English and maths. Reasons given for this were about being prepared for future vocational life:

> A vehicle electrician earns more, and to learn electrics you have to learn maths.   (Roger, interview, January 2009)

> My first choice was the Electricity programme, but I didn't have the grades, I want to keep my options open.
> (Dave, interview, January 2009)

However, we have to consider what gives status in this sub-culture: is it being able to do physical work (as for the lads investigated by Willis 1977), being able to solve problems (as in maths) or make clever statements (as in Swedish)? The observations from the fieldwork rather point to the inter-dependency between competences. For instance, the ability to fix a failing cam-shaft or remedy defects in vehicle electrical systems requires complex skills, involving mental—manual work and practice. The interviews indicate that the complexity was recognised by the students, but they did not seem to recognise and value their own mental work in the vehicle hall and convert it to useful knowledge in the academic subjects. Why constructions of the manual worker appeared to be stronger and why they did not act to blur the division of manual and mental work in their education will be discussed below.

Vehicle masculinities

As mentioned above, all the students in the class and all the teachers except one were male and most were of Swedish background. In the almost entirely male Vehicle Programme environment manual work became closely related to gender, which shaped what could be described as a Vehicle Programme culture.

This culture represented certain notions of appropriate masculinities related to an ambivalent attitude towards theoretical studies. Manual work also was seen to hold high status among the boys, as frequently shown in literature on male working-class identities (Archer, Pratt and Phillips, 2001; Frosh, Phoenix and Pattman, 2002; Arnot, 2004; Smith, 2007; Nixon, 2009).

However, the field work in this class also shows an orientation towards theoretical knowledge among the boys. It seems that they are open to the incorporation of theoretical knowledge into a manually defined masculinity by underlining that theoretical studies are needed to get a job, to earn more, to advance, etc. They could be said to unconsciously elaborate on or to 'modernise' traditional manual masculinities without changing their foundations. This might be an act of meeting new requests from the labour market while holding on to somewhat traditional working class masculinities.

Earlier research in primary school and compulsory school indicates that the gender of the teacher matters little to the students (Lahelma, 2000; Carrington, Francis, Hutchings, Skelton, Read and Hall, 2007), but Francis and Skelton have shown that some male teachers construct themselves as strongly masculine in a way that influences student masculinities (2001, p. 19). In addition, Smith (2007) shows that some male teachers further hegemonic forms of masculinity, not least by emphasising heteronormativity. Holm (2008) argues that this kind of gender idealism and sexism is especially likely to be communicated in informal classroom conversations between students and teachers. In this material there were examples of teachers challenging traditional gender relations in learning situations, but also examples of male teachers reproducing them, mostly through informal jokes:

> *Teacher*: Here we can decide! At home it is your wife.
> *Jörgen*: Or your mum!   (Field notes, March 2009)

In terms of constructions of masculinity there were also comments by the boys on work not done in the vehicle hall as 'sissy' with connotations of homosexuality (which might affect the parameters or kinds of work that they could envisage doing). Reading a book meant a boy could have his sexuality questioned, as noted in previous research (Willis, 1977; Epstein, 1998; Frosh et al, 2002). Especially in the beginning of the school year some of the boys used heteronormativity (cf. Mac an Ghaill, 1994) to challenge each other's positions within the group. For example Paul, might say to Magnus: 'Later on in the shower I'll make you bend over. But of course you'd fancy that, wouldn't you?' (Field notes, September 2008). Many comments were about what they would do to each other in the shower, often to contest the counterparts' heterosexuality. Those comments became increasingly infrequent as the boys seemed to find their positions in the group, and some of those most active in giving comments dropped out. Disruptive behaviour such as Paul's has been noted as a self-worth protection strategy by Jackson (2002, p. 47), who argues that students, particularly boys noted for displaying disruptive 'laddish' behaviour, sabotage the efforts of academically oriented peers in order to hide their own lack of ability.

Later in the school year, although such explicit expressions were no longer as strong and frequent as before, heteronormativity persisted throughout the fieldwork and the way to speak was acknowledged by the boys as a part of the Vehicle Programme culture. Those who did not use swear words or sexist language dissociated themselves from this culture, and said when asked by me that they did not want to be stigmatised as a 'vehicle boy'.

Within the Working Environment and Safety course, the teacher touched upon questions related to gender stereotypes and harassment of the opposite sex or those of non-heterosexual orientation. Otherwise it was unusual for teachers to comment on what the boys said. Corrections were usually about being quieter or lowering voices when the language became too rough, containing homophobic or racist remarks. They were seldom concerned with the content of what was being said. Tariq and Jörgen concluded that not commenting on such content supported it as normal and acceptable: 'The teachers do not do anything when someone says nigger or something. The teacher should say that it is not OK to use such language' (Tariq, interview) and 'When teachers do not do anything it is seems like they do not understand that it is wrong.' (Jörgen, field notes, cf. Francis and Skelton, 2001, p. 18).

These comments point to a kind of Vehicle Programme culture that was difficult for Tariq and Jörgen to challenge and influence without teacher support, in line with conclusions by Nayak and Kehily (1996, in Frosh et al., 2002, p. 175) that racist and homophobic performances are used by young men to 'give substance to masculinity as well as constructing themselves as masculine'. Both Tariq and Jörgen concluded that discriminative talk is difficult to handle on your own. 'You can't be the only one saying that it's not OK to say nigger and such, because if you were, something would happen to you.' (Tariq, interview).

The physical school

The fact that the vehicle building was some distance from the main building had both positive and negative implications for the Vehicle boys. The geographical isolation enabled the development of a certain kind of culture with closeness to mentors but distance from peers on other programmes. This included remoteness from central decision-making, both formal, as in the students' council, and informal as they rarely (if ever) bumped into the head teacher or other key persons, thus reducing their possibilities to exercise influence. The geographical distance also worked as a barrier to teacher support and student health care.

As an example, the school had installed TV-sets to show the latest news and provide information about matters like students' council meetings, the day's lunch, special events and teachers who were sick-listed. However, in the vehicle building there were no TV-sets, due to a lack of cable connections between the buildings, and both teachers and students complained that they did not get information that they needed:

> *Per-Åke*: If you had a class council today, or this afternoon, what questions do you think would be brought up?
> *Anders*: Getting a TV-set up here, to see if a teacher is sick and such like, because we do not get that sort of information. Er, and that, I think, to get to know quicker if the teacher is sick.
>
> (Interview, February 2009)

The problems linking the TV-sets and influence were manifested in the boys' attempts to persuade the head teacher to install a TV-set in the vehicle building, and the reduced possibilities for them to exert influence, since they lacked information the TV-sets provided.

> At a meeting the head teacher says that he will look into the possibility of installing a TV-set in the vehicle building. It is the boys that raise the question and after the head teacher says he will look into it no more questions are raised about the TV-set. They then moved forward with the meeting.   (Field notes, September 2008)

> A discussion about the TV-sets is raised. The head teacher's investigation has taken time and the boys are not satisfied, mostly because of lack of

information about a frequently sick-listed teacher. Their mentor agrees to call the administration every morning to see if any of the boys' teachers are sick-listed and have not been replaced by a substitute teacher. Later the same day I asked Ruben about the TV-set, and if the head teacher had informed them about what will happen. Ruben said that the head teacher had not come to inform them, but the group of boys had met him in the dining hall a couple of times and complained that nothing had happened. (Field notes, November 2008)

I asked Jörgen if he had heard anything about the TV-set. He said that he had met the head teacher: 'I talked with him down by the main building. But he only, you know, looked at me as if to say 'Aren't you finished yet?' He couldn't care less. I guess that we have to write something for him to read.' In other words they have not had an explanation about why no TV-set has been installed. (Field notes, May 2009)

Since the boys did not get information distributed through the TV-sets, they missed out on special events, such as performances in the assembly hall and collective sport activities. Further, and more importantly in relation to influence, they did not get information about students' council meetings. Not being given information gave a feeling of not being important enough to be given information and not being part of the school as a whole.

Education about influence

No teaching about formal influence occurred during the observation period, either as exercised through class and student councils, or as exercised through, for instance, club or trade union activities, except for the efforts of a single teacher, Ola, in a single, specific context. Ola had personal experience of work outside school, and trade union activities for several years. The teacher's background is a factor that Lindberg (2003c) has noted as important for addressing work-related issues, and Ola often used his experience to describe how trade unions had successfully wrought changes. Notably, in interviews the vehicle students showed more awareness of trade union work than students in the social science class, and Ola probably played a role in this, since he often mentioned his own union work. However the students' own working class background was probably also important, since (for instance) research by Öhrn (1998, 2004) indicates that working class youths are more collectively oriented than middle class youths.

The vehicle students also mentioned parents being active in unions, which social science students did not.

During the school year maths became a big issue. The maths teacher was often on sick-leave and many of the boys' lessons in maths were cancelled. In the spring one of the students, Jörgen, said between lessons that they had missed more than a third of their lessons. Much of this was due to school policy; the first day a teacher was home from work there was no substitute teacher and the school did not have a supply pool from which teachers could be asked to fill in at short notice. One day during the autumn Ola acted on this by changing the schedule and educated the boys in how to exercise influence:

> During the autumn the problems about the maths lessons had come up and Ola was aware of the situation. One day the maths teacher had not showed up and the boys sat and waited for the teacher to come. When the teacher did not come some of them went down to the main building to see if she was going to come, and after a while they returned and said that the school administration said that the teacher was not sick-listed and should turn up, but she did not. The next lesson is a theoretical lesson in Vehicle Mechanics. When Ola, who will be the teacher, comes the boys are very frustrated. They walk up to him, complaining about the situation. Ola says: 'Hey, remember that it is not the maths teacher's fault! Everyone can get sick. Then it is the school's responsibility to replace her with a substitute teacher' ... 'We should have a class meeting.' (…) Immediately when they settled down in the classroom Ola starts to educate the boys about how to call a formal meeting. It follows the routine that is usually adopted in union meetings, choice of chair, secretary, persons to check minutes and vice persons to cover the positions. Jörgen is chosen as chair and Magnus as vice chair. (…)
>
> Ola highlights the strength of collective actions: 'If you go one by one down to the head teacher, he will probably not take any notice. A meeting protocol is a strong marker of collective determination.' Ola also refers to successful actions of the students' council, such as when a few years previously the school had decided to make students pay for lunch, but the students' council acted to remove the fee. All of a sudden it seems that Magnus has realised that he was voted to be vice chair and asks: 'What does a chair do?' The other boys laugh, but Ola calms them down and says: 'It is a good question. The chair calls and leads meetings, and

keeps order.' (…) Ola gives an example of how a protocol may appear. He repeats, several times, the importance of writing a protocol. He also repeats that they should not tell the head teacher that it was he who taught them this and helped them with their formulations. He says that he has done this before and it got him into trouble with the head teacher. (…) At the end of the lesson the secretary Ruben is given responsibility for transcribing his notes and giving them to Jörgen, who will be the one who gives the protocol to the head teacher. Ruben never finalised a protocol and the process ended with some students coincidentally meeting the head teacher in the dining hall and telling him about the situation.

(Field notes, November 2008).

The teacher here plays an important role in educating the students about formal routes of influence and decisions. He highlights the value of acting collectively to exercise influence. This is important for the boys as being, i.e. their present, but also for their becoming. The teacher repeating that educating students about influence has got him into trouble, reveals a school structure that does not encourage teachers to educate students to participate in decision routes.

However, during the year nothing changed to compensate the boys for their lost lessons. The problem was postponed to the following term. However, the head teacher said that he was not sure that anything would be changed since by the end of the year the boys had been absent from, on average, sixty per cent of their math lessons (from field notes, May 2009). This raises questions about cause and effect, i.e. did the students' absenteeism rise because of the absence of the teacher, or because of a lack of interest by the students, as the head teacher implied? It is also interesting to compare this response to the example presented in chapter four where the Natural Science Programme students were not allowed to slow the pace. The Vehicle Programme students wanted to speed up their maths education but nothing was done. The boys asked for more maths lessons, which seemingly contradicts their saying that bookish work was sissy, but also could be understood as strengthening the argument that the boys were elaborating traditional manual masculinities.

The system of not deploying a replacement on the first day of a teacher's illness would inevitably affect the performance of students in any subject, but mathematics is especially crucial, since passing the subject is essential for entry into many professional and academic avenues, and is a key criterion of success in the educational system (Turmo, 2004; Lidegran, 2009). Many of the students in the Vehicle class—especially those who barely passed in compulsory school—expressed that the bar was too high for them. In upper secondary school, when they did not get the help they received previously, and this deficit was exacerbated by not having the lessons they were entitled to, they chose not to go to lessons. This response can therefore be seen as an alternative to influence. They chose a silent protest, consciously or unconsciously, of withdrawing from the lessons. This also corresponds with notes by Öhrn (2002a, 2002b) and Weis (1990) that in contemporary schooling (compared to earlier suggestions) boys are less likely to display open resistance.

Something changed, however, after the class meeting in which Ola taught the class about strategies for exercising influence. The boys spoke of the problem in more general terms, as a problem of the school rather than of the teacher. Before the meeting, the boys might say things like: 'Where were you the last lesson?' (Field note), but later they made comments such as: 'Why did we not get a substitute teacher for the last lesson?' or 'Have they looked at the possibilities to put an information-TV up here?' (Field notes). In Bernstein's terms, rather than seeing the problem as local, specific and context-dependent (horizontal), there seemed to have been some changes towards seeing it as systematically structured and hierarchically organised (vertical). They saw the teacher in the vertical hierarchy of the school structure and held the head teacher instead of the subject teacher responsible for the cancellation of classes.

Becoming

As pointed out above, the boys asked for more English, Maths and Swedish teaching in order to be able to influence their future, by creating possibilities for freedom of choice. Knowledge of English etc. is recognised as essential for the ability to influence career choice, develop economic freedom and develop personal knowledge as a form of capital. To achieve this the boys asked for an education that gave them more, for example more support in lessons or more teacher time. This will be explored in relation to the boys becoming below.

Content in the characteristic subjects of the Vehicle Programme

When analysing observations of a group of travel agency students using Bernstein's concepts, Gamble (2006) gave concrete examples of education in a vertical rather than a horizontal discourse:

> I was struck by the skilful manner in which the lecturer led the students
> to understand not only how to fill in a particular flight voucher but also to
> grasp the general rules that helped them to distinguish between different
> kinds of information. This was (---) clearly an occupational programme,
> but the lecturer understood the knowledge base and taught his students
> how to reason rather than just how to fill in forms.
>
> (Gamble, 2006, p. 100)

The content was, in other words, not only of the particular but also spoken about in general terms. In the following section the characteristic subjects of the Vehicle Programme are discussed in terms of influence and both context-dependent and context-independent knowledge.

The vehicle students' mentor also taught all the character subjects of the Vehicle Programme, and the boundaries when one subject course ended and another started were not always clear. In addition, at any given time one student may do work associated with the Vehicle Electronics course while another did Vehicle Repairs and Service work, in other words, the subjects had weak classification.

In the beginning of the school year the teacher started courses by assembling the class in an area of the vehicle hall where there was a white board and school desks. Those courses were often safety courses. Later, since they did not always have enough material, such as customers' cars, electrical circuit boards and so on, different students did their work in different courses at the same time, so it was difficult for the teacher to arrange full group lectures or discussions. The textbook, manuals and instructions from the teacher for small groups or individuals were then the students' sources of information. The students were evaluated through individual tests, on a computer by ticking boxes, through textbook tasks, and by visual observations by the teacher of practical tasks, for example making a lamp glow by connecting leads:

> It was Nick's turn to be examined. He walked into the room that was
> used for examinations and sat down at the computer. I could see the
> questions through the glass pane into the room. Most were designed
> as multiple-choice questions and Nick responded by ticking the boxes
> that he thought were right. Some questions involved singling out the
> right thing in a picture. It could be a picture of an engine and then Nick
> would pinpoint the right part by pointing with the mouse. (---) Nick

comes out of the room with a computer printout in his hand. It says that he got seventy-six per cent right. He shows it to his friends and the teacher congratulates him. I ask Nick what is needed for a Pass and he answers seventy per cent.

(Field notes, February 2009)

The structure of the lessons, with students working on different tasks at the same time using different sources of information and evaluation forms made it difficult to discuss work in general terms. Instructions had to be brief since the teacher often needed to help other students who were waiting, hence instructions were also mostly particular rather than general. In addition, the evaluation by ticking boxes and of results rather than processes made it difficult to raise discussions about reasoning and the evaluation of facts and skills rather than knowledge. Young (2008, p. 170) argues:

> ... the vocational curriculum always has (or should have) two purposes: providing access to the (disciplinary) knowledge that is transforming work, and acquiring job-specific skills and knowledge. The former purpose relies on context-independent knowledge, whereas the latter will be context-specific and related to specific sectors and work places.

The teacher seemed to be aware of this:

> The students break up to work in the vehicle hall. Ola [the teacher] and I follow them a few steps behind. Ola says:'To be a good vehicle mechanic one needs to be able to think abstractly. It is clearly visible that those that are good at maths become good mechanics. Even writing is good when it comes to abstract work in the mechanical field'.

(Field notes, April 2009)

This statement breaks the mental-manual distinction. However, the pedagogic structures (framing of time, resources such as working material, reliance on the textbook, evaluation forms) worked against the development and communication of context-independent knowledge. Hence the students were, if we follow Young's argument, to some extent excluded from knowledge they needed to influence transformation of their working conditions.

Swedish

Karlsson (2009) and Lindberg (2003a) have noted that vocational education involves reading and communicative practice, in addition to manual work practice and the boys observed in this research wanted to influence their careers and were aware that their future profession had higher requirements for language skills than it had previously. For example, in one Swedish lesson the boys had to write down what they thought were the most important elements of their education, and if they wanted more or less of anything:

> Most important, I think, is to learn at least one more language than Swedish and English, most of the manuals are in English or another language.   (Dave, Swedish textbook task, January 2009)

> My goal is to be a vehicle mechanic, so I think that is important. But to manage that, you also have to handle English and Swedish, to understand terms.   (Roger, Swedish textbook task, January 2009)

> You need to read books. There will always be new technologies.
>   (Nick, Swedish textbook task, January 2009)

In Sweden—just as Young (2006) described for England—vocational education has been adapted to employers' demands regarding what should be counted as vocational knowledge, and thus what should be in the curriculum. Today there is an explicit goal to integrate core subjects with character subjects for the programme to create a meaningful whole. Some school projects have progressed a long way towards such integration, and Lindberg (2003b, 2003c) argues that interaction between subjects is more successful when the core subject-teacher has experience of working life outside school. At the school in this study few core subject teachers had such experience. The boys' Swedish teacher, however, was an exception. He was newly employed at the school and had experience of working life, but had not yet had time to establish clear cooperation with the teachers of the Vehicle Programme.

The content of the subject Swedish that was presented to the boys had a traditional approach, with a focus on cultural aspects of Swedish, i.e. mainly fictional texts were read. However, there were also texts that were adapted to the Vehicle Programme, like the textbook *Blickpunkt—fordon [Centre-stage—*

vehicles] (Hedencrona and Smed-Gerdin, 2007) that has been produced for use on the Vehicle Programme. The publisher's description of the textbook on their website conceptualises the kind of reader the publisher thinks the vehicle student is likely to be:

> Centre-stage vehicles has 104 pages and is in full colour. The book contains plenty of photographs that illustrate the texts, making the content easy and inviting.
> (webbshop.gleerups.se/se/gymnasieskola_and_vuxenutbildning,
> Available 5 October 2010: My translation)

The vehicle student reader is conceptualised as one who wants easy, inviting reading rather than texts that challenge him or her to reflect and analyse. It is also notable that the paragraph mentions 'full colour' and 'plenty of photographs' before saying anything about the text. This may conflict with both the boys' notion of wanting more out of their education and earlier research on vocational programmes indicating that simplification and trivialisation of content in core subjects is counter-productive. When one makes content too easy, students seem to lose interest (Berglund, 2009, p. 211).

To my knowledge, the students were never asked if they wanted to use the textbook with vehicle-related texts, and they never opposed reading the texts. On the other hand, between lessons and in interviews some of them expressed views that education on the Vehicle Programme was a bit uniform: 'Everything we do is about cars, sometimes it feels good to do something else,' (Ulf, interview, March 2009) and some stated that vehicles were not their main interest 'The Vehicle Programme wasn't my first choice you know. It was the electricity programme. But I thought, if I start here, I might be able to change later' (Dave, field note, September 2008).

In other words, Swedish was classified or heavily biased towards vehicle-related Swedish, not because it was what the boys wanted, nor because it met the curricular criteria of fostering 'language skills *and* understanding of other cultural patterns', but due to a presumption that Vehicle Programme students want to read texts relating to vehicles (cf. Keddie, 1971; Beach, 1999b; Korp, 2006). The unidirectional texts in both narratives and genres make it difficult to train students in what Norlund names different 'critical reading activities' (2009). Instead, the education becomes shallowly uniform, with little connection to general subject knowledge or academic nature.

These observations are consistent with findings by Norlund (2009) in an analysis of differences between textbooks said to be adapted for academic and vocational programmes, in terms of the way questions are asked. Questions in textbooks designed for vocational programmes generally require users to seek fact-based answers (horizontal discourse) in the text while questions in textbooks for academic programmes generally require students to compare and analyse material (vertical discourse). Following Norlund's (2009) analytical model the same can be said about questions posed in the textbook *Blickpunkt.*

Curriculum course goals emphasise that students should receive education that is relevant both for their *chosen study orientation* and their role as *citizens of the society*, and it is specifically stipulated that both *non-fiction* and *literary texts* should be used (Course goals, Swedish A). This research indicates that in practice there is a heavy bias towards the students' chosen study orientation rather than their role as citizens of the society, and subordination of the students, through the boys being prepared only to participate in horizontal discourse. This will not help them strengthen their position in society.

The tasks in their textbook focused on learning facts and skills rather than reflections in general terms, which Hultin (2008, p. 105) has pointed out is a tradition in vocational training, in contrast to academic programmes that focus more on the latter. Following the 1994 curriculum reform there was a shift towards trying to even out segregation due to socioeconomic factors, but even though the vehicle students have the same syllabus, for core subjects, as those attending academic programmes differences still seem to persist.

Lundahl (2008) and Nylund (2010), who analyse the coming upper secondary reform to be implemented in 2011 point at a break with the traditions of integrating educational routes. It will divide vocational and academic education, and the required core subjects on the vocational programmes will be reduced, which means that the ambitions for these programmes will be lowered and aligned with those of corresponding programmes in the other Scandinavian countries. Nylund argues that core subjects such as Swedish will have a weaker role and that the reform maps out specific routes for the students on the vocational programmes to accept a subordinated position in the division of labour and in society as a whole (Nylund, 2010, p. 41, p. 49). Hultin (2008, p. 105) concludes that the reduction in the vocational students' education in Swedish proposed by the reform risks making them unable to meet the demands of employers and to participate in and influence the society. It is therefore interesting to see that the boys asked for more education in core subjects, not less, which the reform proposes.

Being and becoming compared

An important aspect that this research has highlighted is the apparent progressive passivity of the boys. In the beginning of the school year they made several visible attempts to exercise influence, such as giving themselves a new start by going to the maths support sessions, requesting order in the classroom and convening a class meeting to try to influence the head teacher. When the activities were usually unsuccessful it seemed that the boys increasingly rarely tried to influence or talk about trying to influence the order of the school. Thus, events and responses during the initial phase of a programme appear to be important if the school wants to promote student influence.

Collectively considering all of the observations and theoretical perspectives discussed above, education in the Vehicle Programme appears to be largely limited to transmission of reproductive knowledge, giving students little power to reflect, calculate, analyse, draw conclusions and see beyond the Vehicle Programme culture. Furthermore, the Vehicle Programme building is 'cut off' from other students and decision routes, located some five-hundred meters away, and the instruction focuses mainly on manual tasks. This draws attention to homogenisation towards a specific Vehicle Programme culture, but does not reflect the diversity among the boys' interests. During interviews all the boys expressed interest in developing their skills in theoretical subjects and a desire to get, one way or another, more out of their education. The boys were not interested solely in cars or people connected to cars, and to enhance knowledge related to their diverse interests they wanted to develop theoretical, abstract and esoteric competences that Bernstein includes in vertical discourse.

Since 1968, the teaching of vocational students has shifted from apprentice-workplace-based training to school-based education. The time before young people in Sweden are fully integrated into working life has been extended and almost all now go to upper secondary school (see chapter two). The stated motive driving these changes has been that everyone should have access to reflective, analytical and universal knowledge, or what Bernstein calls vertical knowledge. When we look at the practice of the Vehicle Programme, we see that the goals of the reforms have not been fulfilled, since it was local, context-dependent and specific, i.e. relied on horizontal knowledge (Bernstein, 2000, p. 157).

Since we know that primarily working-class youths attend vocational programmes it does not seem sufficient to extend vocational education and base it at school instead of workplaces. If we are serious about fostering social equality, courses should provide space for critical reflection of general principles, or in other words, access to vertical discourse (Bernstein, 2000). This is to appreciate the complexity of the vocational practice in the same manner we do for professional practice (cf. Gamble, 2006; Wheelahan, 2007; Young, 2008). The nature of the class differences between programmes, and the students that take them, still seems to be deeply rooted when the pedagogic practices are examined. The pedagogic practice observed in this research seemed to be strongly oriented towards education for manual work, which denies the boys possibilities to participate in and influence a vertical discourse of powerful knowledge. Furthermore, the reform due to be implemented by the current government seems destined to increase the bias *against* broad citizenship education and preparation for political emancipation (Lundahl et al., 2010; Nylund, 2010).

Lastly, some words about gender. We must be aware of the complexity of definitions of gender relations in culture, not least since gender relations constantly change (Arnot, 2002), which also became visible in this research.

In this text I have argued that the boys in the Vehicle Programme class appear to be dealing with a shift in traditional understandings of masculinity and a dichotomy being constructions of what it means to be a 'real man' and official pedagogic practice. This dichotomy could be embodied in one and the same boy, who at one time could oppose school, as a good representative of the traditional working class lad, but on other occasions ask for more core subject knowledge, more lesson time, order in classroom or access to student support. In other words, he could be said to be a boy who goes beyond the traditional manual masculinities you would expect to find in this context through his orientation towards the academic subjects. In addition, peer relations seemed to sustain traditional gender stereotypes, while an orientation towards theoretical knowledge, fostered by a desire to get a good job, earn more and promote future advancement could also be discerned.

Chapter 8

Can this be called democracy?

Marianne Dovemark

Introduction

This chapter is about the Chisel and Quill classes of the Individual Programme at Currant Upper-secondary school in Lake City. The Individual Programme (for a general description, see chapter two) is predominantly characterised as a low-status programme nationally, and this appears to apply to the programme offered at Currant Upper. This chapter describes how such a subordinate position affects students' possibilities of exerting influence. However, it also highlights occasions when the students were seen as a resource for change and acted with both power and strength.

The chapter is based upon long-term ethnographic observations and interviews, which have been used to examine how aspects of democracy develop in practice within new policies of personalised and individual learning (cf. Beach and Dovemark, 2007). One of the main features of the fieldwork has been flexibility, with regard to time and visits in the field (Jeffrey and Troman, 2004). I had access to the field whenever I wanted during the school year, that is I could 'pop in, whenever', as one teacher expressed it. On average, I visited the school two full or half days a week from August 2008 to the end of June 2009.

The analyses are based on participant observations, formal interviews, field interviews and various kinds of artefacts found in the field (Hammersley and Atkinson, 1995; Willis, 2000). The main focus has been on students during lessons. To observe practices and processes in the education of Chisel students, I followed all twent-two of the students in the current class during their everyday life in school and the school's mechanical workshop. For practical reasons I could not attend their work in the kitchen—the other site of practical training (see below). For corresponding observations of Quill students I focused particularly on twelve students, who I followed in various constellations depending on the subjects they were studying. The selected students belonged to three different so-called home groups, and they were selected because they had relatively large numbers of lessons per week, and thus were fairly often at school. Home-groups are an administrative group of pupils not a study-group.

Before lessons started and during the morning break, I followed the staff into the staff rooms. In early stages I found this interesting and fruitful, as the teachers discussed the students quite frequently during these periods. I also had the opportunity to simply 'be around' the students during breaks and free time. I spent time at the cafeteria, in the assembly room and in corridors. I decided not to encroach in some areas, for example the 'smoking areas', as I regarded these as students' 'private zones'. Furthermore, I participated in three excursions and twelve planning dialogues between students and teachers. The formal interviews with the students took place in April and May 2009, and those with the staff in May and June the same year. Twenty-four students (17-18 years old), ten teachers, the head master and three instructors were interviewed. All interviews were audio recorded and transcribed. The present chapter is based on transcriptions of the interviews and field notes.

The Individual programme at Currant Upper—an isolated programme

Lake City is a medium-sised town with around 55,000 inhabitants. The school had approximately 2,000 students, and hence is regarded as a big school in Sweden. It offered more than twenty different programmes, some academically and others vocationally oriented. The Individual Programme offered maths, Swedish/Swedish as a second language, English and social sciences. One hundred and twenty of the students, approximately six per cent of the total, at Currant Upper attended the Individual Programme in August 2008 when the fieldwork began, of whom twenty-two were registered at Chisel, and the rest at Quill. Approximately a quarter of the students had an immigrant background. All newly arrived immigrants in Lake City were placed on the Individual Programme for their first studies in the Swedish language.

The two different parts of the Individual Programme had different characteristics. Chisel had a marked practical orientation, including compulsory manual activities in a mechanical workshop and a kitchen located within the school premises. Quill was said 'more theoretically oriented' (Sten, teacher) and its activities were located in a former industrial building some four hundred metres from the main school. Chisel activities were located in an industrial area in the eastern outskirts of Lake City several kilometres away. Barbed wire fences surrounded the site, hence Chisel was even more isolated from other programmes in terms of locations and staff than Quill.

Seven out of ten teachers of the Individual Programme had a background as a preschool teacher. The Chisel staff also included four instructors, working in the kitchen and mechanical workshop, who had no pedagogical education. Although some of the teachers at the school could teach elements of both the Individual Programme and National Programmes, none of the teachers attached to the latter participated in the education of either Quill or Chisel students. Moreover, due to their geographical isolation Individual Programme students (especially Chisel students) tended to miss events such as sport activities and activities in the assembly hall, e.g. student council meetings.

As the name indicates, the Individual Programme at Currant Upper was strongly officially focused on the individual student, but in practice the main feature was a strong focus on manual or vocational work, but without the purposeful connection to working life which is a key feature of the Vocational Programmes (Olofsson and Wadensjö, 2007). Preparation for further studies was clearly oriented to specific Vocational Programmes, in particular Hotel, Restaurant and Catering, Business and Administration and the Vehicle Programmes—rather than the academic programmes, the programmes oriented towards new media and aesthetics, and the Individual Programme. This dichotomy was clearly evident in an examination of forty websites, in which various municipalities (including Lake City) and schools presented their individual programmes. Thirty-seven showed pictures of students doing carpentry, mechanics or cooking.

The text of Lake City's presentation (typically), stated that: 'The Individual Programme is intended for those of you who want to prepare for continued studies and study on the basis of your own qualifications, and for skilled work. You get vocational guidance and social and professional training. It is also good for those of you who need to work with your motivation and identity'.

All presentations showed a strong emphasis on skilled work, motivation and personal development. Targeting students' recognised 'needs', this marketing thus tried to convince students to accept 'who and what you are' and 'take responsibility for their own redemption' (Dovemark, 2004a, 2004b, 2008; Beach and Dovemark, 2007, 2009). The next section takes a closer look at the students who attend the Individual programme in general and the programme at Currant Upper in particular.

Who attends the Individual Programme?

Research indicates that there is a strong relationship between students' socioeconomic background and study results (Olofsson and Wadensjö 2007, p. 55-57). Accordingly, as mentioned before (chapter two), students attending the Individual Programme come predominantly from homes without academic traditions (Broady and Gustafson, 2000; Svensson 2001, 2006). When asked about their parents' occupations, nineteen of the twenty-four interviewed students mentioned typical working-class jobs such as lorry driver, care assistant, industrial labourer, plumber or painter, and several had parents who were currently unemployed, on sick leave or on social security pensions. One student told me his father was working for a newspaper. I later found out that it was *Faktum*, a paper sold by homeless people.

One common reason why students end up in the individual programme is that they lack sufficient grades in the core subjects or knowledge of the Swedish language. The Swedish National Agency for Education (2007, p. 5) describes the students on the Individual Programme not only as 'unauthorised', 'unmotivated' or 'new Swedes' but also as 'disrupters', 'swappers' or 'waiters' (see also chapter two). Willy, one of the teachers of the studied programme at Currant Upper characterised the enrolled students as follows:

> [The circumstances] differ a lot ... with social barriers, depression ... problems at home, things that made them stay at home a lot [during compulsory school] ... I would say there are roughly four groups ... those who are here because of social problems ... students who have serious learning disabilities, you know reading and writing disabilities and concentration difficulties ... and of course all newly arrived foreigners who are here to learn Swedish, some of them are very well educated, others are illiterate ... and the last group are those who haven't got enough credit points for a desired [national] programme or those who have left a [national] programme for one reason or another.
>
> (Field notes Quill, September 2008)

Lydia, another teacher, explained that the students who attended the Individual Programme were those who 'the secondary school hasn't coped with well'. She pointed out that there were 'hundreds of reasons' why students ended up on the programme and exemplified them, as follows: 'everything from medical conditions like ADHD and anorexia' to reasons concerning 'lack of help and support (during compulsory school)'. The strong focus on different diagnoses was something that struck me during my fieldwork. A majority of the staff, though with some strong exceptions, used neuro-psychological explanations like ADHD, ADD and Asperger's syndrome:

> In the staff group there was then a fairly intense discussion about the reasonableness of some diagnoses. As before, the staff has differing views about this ... They are split on the usefulness of diagnoses [ADHD, etc.] of students, even though most of them advocate their use. Anders, for instance, stated emphatically that it is more a question of resources: 'The school has been drained of resources in recent decades ... diagnosis hysteria becomes a way for schools to acquire more resources'.
>
> (Field notes Quill, August 2008)

The students were mainly described as being at risk of poor school performance, without addressing the nature of schooling itself. The problem was said to be that the children 'at risk' had failed to adapt and cope with the requirements of the school system, or poor motivation was blamed for their performance deficits. The students or their homes were seen as poor. Such deficit frameworks detract attention from circumstances that genuinely result in students being put 'at risk', such as low expectations and demands (Persson, 2005; Angus, 2009). In contrast, most of the studied students attributed their school failures to practices of their former teachers and schoolmates, rather than deficits in their ability to learn, and did not consider that they had cognitive difficulties. Like the students observed by Henriksson (2004), they argued instead that it was always their behaviour that had been noted and focused upon during compulsory school.

Wendy was one of these students. She attended the Individual programme because she had not passed in English and religious education; not because of 'lack of ability', she said, but because she 'got a new teacher in form nine who didn't like her' and 'dropped her marks'. The relationship between her and the former teacher had become so debilitating that Wendy refused to go to lessons and hand in work, a strategy that resulted in non-passing grades. She illustrated how vulnerable students may be within the Swedish school system (see also Osbeck, Holm and Wernersson, 2003; Swedish National Agency for Education, 2009a; Swedish Schools Inspectorate, 2010). A great majority of the interviewed students told me similar stories. Several of them found that there should be an obvious right to criticise teachers when they 'put things offensively' (Linda) or when they 'malign students' (Pia), but with very few exceptions they found that it was impossible to criticise teachers, for example concerning marking, working forms and lack of help (see also Öhrn, 2005):

> You really should be able to say what you think [to the teacher] and it's important to be able to talk openly at school ... without teachers getting bitter and bad-tempered ... you will be punished [if you say what you think] ... we are forced to go to school for the first nine years and if we don't get the help we need, we are still forced to go there ... we really should get all the help we need.   (Interview, Niklas, May 2009)

Cassandra was another student who told me about her relations to her former teachers: 'I could only talk to one teacher ... but not the others ... if you said you felt insulted or bullied they just said 'What?' [and looked surprised] ... all [other teachers] behaved disinterestedly and ingenuously ... they really didn't care'. Many serious accusations against their former teachers came up one day when the Chisel students were given a task to describe what they would see if they went back as 'a fly on the wall at their former [compulsory] school' (Inez, teacher). Accusations, such as 'Unfair treatment and teachers' (Rina); 'Fighting and bullying' (Andy) and even sexual harassment from teachers were experienced. Such accusations needed to be discussed and tackled, but according to the students it was impossible to criticise teachers and these questions were seldom on the agenda. To these students, school itself was obviously the problem. There is a 'conflict between what school offers, and what students claim they need or desire' (Henriksson, 2004, p. 157-158). The students' picture was actually strengthened by staff. Several of them stated, like Ulla below, that the perceptions of students held by compulsory school and Individual Programme teachers did not correspond:

> The reports [from staff at compulsory school] don't correspond [with our experience]. You don't believe it's the same youngsters ... it's really strange ... The negative image you often get ... it doesn't correspond at all ... it's rather the opposite [the students are very nice].
>   (Field notes Chisel, April 2009)

To summarise, a majority of students on the studied Individual Programme had bad experiences of compulsory school. They described a lack of help and even insulting behaviour from former teachers (see also Osbeck et al., 2003). They also found it difficult to criticise teachers.

Perceptions of the students on the Individual Programme

The stigmatising of Individual Programme students—'IP students' (Lina) became apparent even before the fieldwork began, during the information meeting for students and their parents in the spring:

> About fifty people (young people and their parents) are sitting in the cafeteria. The headmaster greets the visitors and starts by informing the students and their parents about the Individual Programme. He says that it is intended to 'qualify students for a National Programme; the goal is that the students qualify for attending a National Programme after one year here on the Individual Programme'. He tells the visitors that the students will be taught Maths, English, Swedish and Social Sciences at contemporary school level: 'Our starting point is every student's own situation and every student's needs'. All the visitors are quiet and attend to the headmaster. The headmaster points out that the Individual Programme is an 'upper secondary school programme'. He also informs the visitors that manual work is included for all students. Repeatedly, he points out that it is all about 'freedom under responsibility'; 'adult responsibility'; that students have responsibility for their own studies and are supposed to 'take active part in the lessons'. He also informs the visitors that the school welfare team, the 'school welfare officer and nurse will always be there, supporting' the students. He turns to the youngsters: 'It is up to you! We will give all the support we can! We will try to guide you. I've got the responsibility for that'. Than the headmaster turns to the parents: 'Much is done to try to find out what your son or daughter really needs'.   (Field notes Quill, June 2008)

The headmaster's point of departure was a firm conviction that the young people were 'fed up with school' (interview, headmaster) and were in need of support and help from the school welfare office. Even the teachers taking part in the information meeting emphasised the importance of starting from 'wherever every student, he or she, is' as one teacher put it. They assured the listeners that as teachers they were 'tremendously flexible' and the main aim was to 'meet the student's needs'. Even though the principal and the teachers were keen to describe the programme as a positive alternative, the whole information meeting bore the stamp of 'the loser's choice'. It was expressed in terms of statements like 'this is good for weak students' (Sten, teacher) and the assumption that the students thought that 'school was boring and fed up with it' (headmaster).

Despite the political aims to provide equal conditions within upper secondary education, a range of studies indicate that the programmes differ in recruitment patterns and status (Broady and Börjeson, 2006; Svensson, 2001, 2006; Broady and Gustafsson, 2000; Beach, 1999b; Lidegran, 2009; Norlund, 2009) and that the Individual Programme has the lowest status (Hultqvist, 2001; Johansson, 2009). Furthermore, although students are supposed to be prepared for participation in, and to take responsibility for the rights and obligations that characterise a democratic society (Ministry of Education and Research, 1994, p. 3), there are important shortcomings in its contribution to fostering a more just and equitable society.

Here it is important to clarify that I do not refer to students on the programme as being 'disadvantaged'; they have been placed in situations of disadvantage. Disadvantage is economically, politically and socially constructed by operations of financial, labour and housing markets through government economic and public policies. Hence, instead of applying the notion of 'disadvantage' to individual people with individual deficits or problems, people should be seen as being beset by problems that are related to structural and institutional issues. Communities, schools and programmes are social arenas in which wider social relations, culture and politics are played out and mediated through the everyday lived experiences and views of human agents. Through subtle and uncertain interactions of agency and structures, social groups and individuals come to 'embody, mediate and enact the operations and results of unequal power' (Willis and Trondman, 2000, p. 10).

Actually the students had no choice, they were placed on the Individual Programme for one reason or another, and it soon became obvious that the staff's assumption about them being 'fed up with school' was far from correct. I met several students who said they were, at least at the beginning of the school year, full of energy and ready to tackle their studies as quickly as possible to pass. But they gradually fell into a slow pace when expectations and demands were placed at a low level. Several of the teachers seemed to see the students as persons 'with special needs' (Inez) in the first place rather than ambitious learners (see also chapter five). This theme is further discussed below, but first the organisation of teaching in the Quill and Chisel sections of the programme is briefly outlined.

The organisation of teaching

The Quill students were organised into groups of eight to ten, depending on the subject. Thus, a student could belong to several different groups, even though they belonged to one 'home group' with one 'contact teacher'. Students came and went according to their individual schedules, which included five to twenty lessons a week, depending on how many subjects they had to study and if they chose extra lessons in computer studies. Because of the different schedules the students ended up in many different constellations, which 'made it hard to get to know each other' (Marie student). Moreover, students had individual manual practice during different days, which made it even more difficult to find common venues. The students at Quill came to a lesson or two, had a long break, went for practical work, then another lesson or went home. A picture appeared of a loose organisation with few fixed groups and few opportunities to create common collective arenas for socialisation.

For Chisel students, the organisation was quite different. The group of twenty-two students was stable in the sense that they were all in school from eight a.m. to two p.m. every day. They started with a common breakfast, had a couple of lessons or manual work in the kitchen or the mechanical workshop, with a coffee break at ten-thirty, another lesson up to noon, then lunch, and the day finished with some more lessons or manual work. The organisation and furnishing signalled strong individual-based teaching:

> At the end of the corridor was a room to the right, screened off with big glass partitions on two sides. The room had a desk at one long side, screened off into three working places, each approximately one metre wide. Each working place had a computer and above each computer was a small shelf. In front of each computer was a chair. The corridor opened up into a big room, where there were a further seven screened-off working places to the right and three to the left. The working places all faced the walls and signalled individual personalised learning. They looked like cubicles. Some of them were decorated with pictures of lorries ... others had photos of musicians or drawings ... There were another three rooms.

Two of them contained more screened off working places, four in one and six in the other. (Field notes Chisel, August 2008)

Joint briefings and lectures were rare occurrences, instead textbooks provided the main structure for the courses. The exceptions were mainly in Quill Social Sciences lessons. A kind of 'own work' (Dovemark, 2004a, 2008; Nilsson, 2002) and personalised learning (Beach and Dovemark, 2007, 2009), characterised by weak framing of space and time, is common within Swedish schools. Thus, I did not expect to encounter a pedagogic practice dominated by lectures, not least since a key element of the programme's rationale was individual teaching, but I was struck by the fact that the classroom was seldom used as a collective arena.

Teachers are, of course, constrained by the current education policy regime, and the emphasis on tests and performativity has had a narrowing effect on educational practice (Ball, 2003; Jeffrey and Woods, 1998). Questions and problems about everyday life as part of the educational process are pushed into the background. Tests define what is officially important within the education system as a whole, including the studied Individual Programme. Tests were the most important tool to attain the main goal for the whole programme, namely to pass to become eligible for a National Programme (Swedish National Agency for Education, 2001). The teaching practice, in both the Quill and Chisel sections, was mainly based on individual schedules. The students studied on their own, aided by teaching material which provided the contents, focusing on learning facts and skills rather than on reflections and analysis in general terms (see also Norlund, 2009). Students also decided when they wanted to take a test:

> Four students are in the kitchen, seven in the mechanical workshop ...
> eight students are sitting at their 'cubicles', Lisa and John are sitting at
> the big table. The teacher tells the students to 'continue their work'. Susie
> opens her novel and starts reading; Jim wants to do maths and picks
> up his books, Sara gets her pre-produced stencils, the others start their
> computers. John and Lisa ask the teacher if they can 'try to do their tests'
> in maths and English. (Field notes Chisel, April 2009)

The pedagogic practice was characterised by weak framing (Bernstein, 1975, 1990, 2003), with a content focused on textbooks' fixed subjects and skills as the structuring principles. The weak framing of the organisation and strong focus on freedom of choice gave an impression of extensive opportunity to exercise influence, but a quite different impression emerged when analysing the observations and interviews, as discussed in the following section.

Influence through freedom of choice

As the name suggests, the Individual Programme was strongly focused on the individual student, with a strong emphasis on personalised education and, as mentioned above, personal schedules were an important part of the practice. The first three weeks of the autumn (and sometimes more) were assigned to arranging these personal schedules. Two teachers at a time met every student for thirty to forty-five minutes of dialogue, the nature of which varied substantially, depending on the teachers involved. Some dialogues focused mainly on family matters and others on the subjects the students wanted to study. Generally the meetings had a strong focus on freedom of choice. Both field notes and journal notes illustrate this pattern, and my own frustration about how the young people were left to their own devices:

> The teachers try to encourage the students by declaring 'we are going to have our starting point from each individual's level and desire. You are going to work out and plan what you want to do, a lot yourself.' The teachers repeat this time and again during the planning meeting. They also clarify that: 'We are not going to force you to do anything'. The starting point seems to be the students' own desires and wishes … but how do the students know what to choose?
>
> (Field notes Quill, September 2008)

The teachers reiterated the ideology of freedom of choice not only during the planning meetings but also during the everyday activities. Statements such as, 'You students have to decide yourselves what you want to learn' (Anders) were frequently made, and journal notes such as: 'The teachers really try hard to meet the students' wishes' indicate the focus on freedom of choice. My own questions reflected my frustration, e.g. 'Is it reasonable? How do the students know what to choose? How informed are the choices they make? Do the students know the consequences of the choices? How does this possibility to exercise 'freedom of choice' and 'voluntariness' affects the young people's future schooling? (Journal notes). Generally the students' choices were not demanding, instead they signalled choices of paths of least resistance.

The possibilities to exert direct influence, like freedom of choice, seemed to affect students' willingness to study adversely. We know, through both Swedish (Beach, 1999b; Dovemark, 2004a, 2004b, 2008; Norlund, 2009; Johansson, 2009) and international (Angus, 2009) studies, that low expectations, boring and irrelevant curricula and lack of respect and encouragement result in low achievements by working-class children. The next part considers the teaching practice more closely.

The teachers' low expectations

The enormous scope for choosing time, space, content etc. (see also Dovemark, 2004a; Hjelmér, Lappalainen and Rosvall, 2010) had counter-productive effects; the demands became low and time after time, as mentioned above, the students seemed to choose the path of least resistance: 'Once again Simon starts a computer game instead of doing his English. Always the same, he seems to avoid it once again.' (Field notes Chisel, February 2009). Moreover, even if students showed high ambitions, at least in the beginning of the school year, they were actually encouraged to reduce them. Mia was one example. During the planning meetings at the start of the school year she told the teachers that she now wanted 'to go for it and study like mad'. The two teachers tried to persuade her to 'ease up a bit'. Instead of encouraging Mia, who wanted to make a new start and get more out of her education (see also chapter seven), they underestimated and trivialised her ambitions. Mia was far from alone in that experience. Tim was another student with high ambitions. The field notes below come from his planning meeting:

> One of the teachers asks Tim: 'You want to have some late mornings, don't you? You want to sleep in the morning? ... When do you want to end [in the afternoon]'? Tim: 'At two ... three ... ' The teacher smiles a bit and says to Tim: 'That sounds a lot, I think that will be too much'.
> (Field note Quill, August 2008)

So, even when a student communicated an ambition to work hard in school, like Tim and Mia, teachers advised them to reduce their ambitions. Their comments seemed to conflict bizarrely with the stated aims of the course, and 'freedom of choice' seemed to be restricted to choices of possibilities to lower the pace and difficulty level, or minimise work. The question is why teachers did not encourage and require the students to study hard in order to be accepted for a National Programme, which was the main official goal for the programme. The practice, both during lessons and during most of the planning dialogues, had a strong focus on private relations rather than on teaching contents (see also chapter six).

The most pronounced examples of teachers slowing down the pace of academic study were in their encouragement of Chisel students to do manual work in the kitchen or mechanical workshop and Quill students to set their own 'training paces':

> 'Everyone has to have a proper training pace. You are probably fed up with schoolwork and it is good for you to do manual work.' The emphasis they placed on manual work was also manifested in changes to students' personal schedules, mostly from academic to manual work.
> (Field notes information meeting, June 2008)

> 09.00 Gathering around the two tables before starting the day's work. Sune, one of the instructors, is as usual taking the floor. One of the students is supposed to be in the mechanical workshop but is ill today. Sune turns to Andy: 'We can't be without your help today. Can you come down [to the mechanical workshop] today?' Andy looks happy and with a broad smile says, 'YES'.   (Field notes Chisel, April 2009)

The most discouraging aspect of this was that Andy only studied one day a week, even though he had not passed in any core subjects. He said this was only because he had 'bad experiences in compulsory school', not because he had 'learning difficulties'. I was struck by the fact that he, and several others, avoided academic work so often during the fieldwork. It was clearly not an important issue within the practice of the Individual Programme.

Students were also habitually constructed and labelled as 'manual'. Expressions like 'I'm a manual person'; 'I'm not theoretically oriented'; 'I like to do things with my hands instead of reading' were frequently heard from both male and female students, although more often from the males (see also chapter seven). The notion and labelling of 'practical or theoretical' was strengthened by teachers time after time:

> Inez (teacher), Andy, Philip and Mia are sitting at the big table and discussing things. Philip raises the question: 'What exactly does it mean

to be smart?' Andy says with emphasis: 'I'm smart in any case!'. Inez gives him an affirmative answer and points out that the concept of 'smart can mean different things'. Then she turns to Andy: 'I'm not smart when it comes to practical things'.   (Field notes Chisel, March 2009)

Students meet different expectations when labelled as 'theoretical' or 'practical'. These distinctions are related practically, theoretically and empirically not only through the overt curriculum but also through the hidden curriculum. The most prevalent are the different demands and expectations placed on students (Beach, 1999b; Dovemark, 2004a, 2004b, 2008; Korp, 2006; Norlund, 2009).

Jonathan, a Chisel student who had passed all subjects but English provides another example. He 'had chosen' to study once a week, and the other days he spent in the mechanical workshop. He had merely one day a week during a whole school year to try to pass in English. He simply refused. I rarely saw him study English. He made a joke out of it and the teachers let him be: 'We can't force him ... Maybe next year he will study. Maybe he will mature next year' (Inez). This raises questions about the factors that allow students such as Jonathan to avoid tackling key elements of the curriculum year after year. One of the major factors was that the everyday pedagogic practice concentrated on the emotional rather than the cognitive content at both the Chisel and Quill sites; it was more important to keep Jonathan in a good mood than to persuade or force him to study English. The ideology of education with a focus on inner motivation, self-regulation, invisible self-governance, personal choice and other self-monitored activities was clearly very strong, and this ideology and practice are very often highly socially reproductive (Dovemark, 2004a, 2004b, 2008; Beach and Dovemark, 2007, 2009).

The example below of 'ducking out' is from an English lesson at the Quill site. The teacher had given the students a task to look up a number of words in a dictionary and write down the translations in Swedish. Approximately ten minutes into the lesson the following exchange occurs:

Leo is looking into space, doing nothing. When the teacher reminds him of the task he looks over the shoulder of Tim, who is sitting next to him, and writes down a word. Leo doesn't look up a single word. The teacher doesn't remark on this and I wonder, once again, what does Leo actually *do* in school? He passes time day after day without doing any schoolwork really ... Another five minutes pass and Leo

calls the teacher and says something in a low voice to her. She nods
to him and he stands up and leaves the room ... He doesn't come back.
(Fieldnotes Quill, February 2009)

When I asked the teacher why Leo went away, she told me that he had
permission to fetch his sweater. Since Leo only had two or three lessons a
day, there would have been plenty of time to get his sweater without wasting
lesson time. Stine, one of the teachers who occasionally raised questions about
'expectations and demands', expressed concern that the students were used to
negotiating in order to avoid tasks they were supposed to do. They were used
to 'these phenomena [processes and behavioural patterns] from earlier school
years,' she said. She added that this was one reason why so many students 'didn't
actually do what they were supposed to and had the capacity to do'.

A substitute teacher, who started teaching at the Quill site in the middle of
the autumn, Stine, was the only teacher who openly questioned the pace and
low demands of the Individual Programme. She tried to put the issue on the
agenda at a working meeting, but was met with a total lack of appreciation by her
colleagues, and the morning after the meeting I encountered a tense atmosphere
and agitation when I entered the Quill staff's room:

> The teachers seem to be distressed and are talking in upset voices. When
> I ask them what's happened, Vera tells me about their working meeting
> yesterday when Stine had questioned their practice [on the Individual
> Programme]. Vera says in an upset voice: 'She [Stine] doesn't know
> anything about our students!'.   (Field notes Quill, October 2008)

Stine did not accept the code of the programme, but did not get support from
her new colleagues when questioning it. Her reaction ended more or less in
isolation, and she then 'went her own way, together with her students, instead of
continuing the discussion as a substitute' (Stine). It turned out that her students
liked her very much, despite her relatively tough demands, or perhaps precisely
because she expected them to manage.

The special educational needs teacher for the Chisel students verified the fact
that students did not perform according to their capacity. When I asked how
many of the twenty-two students enrolled on the Chisel course he believed
had learning difficulties, he said after a moment's thought: 'Maybe four'. An
orientation towards the individual, private and emotional was clearly prioritised,

strongly, over reaching the goals of the core subject courses through high quality studies, together with a lack of academic guidance for future studies.

The scourge of kindness

The programme was the only choice for those students who had not passed in core subjects, but it was also recommended to those who were unsure about what they wanted to do, and/or had failed to adapt to and cope with the requirements of the school system; those who were said to have 'special needs' (Stig, teacher). The programme was expected to have a caring and personality developing character (see also Hultqvist, 2001; Johansson, 2009). Every one of the twenty-four interviewed students told me that they liked their year on the Individual Programme and my field notes repeatedly record that there were hardly ever any quarrels or rows between the teachers and the students, or even between the students themselves. Every single day I wrote field notes such as: 'A nice atmosphere and kind treatment by the teachers'; 'It's incredible! The teachers never seem to raise their voices or lose their temper'; 'The teachers don't even get irritated'; 'Another day in the field with no conflict or aggression'. The breaking-up ceremony at the Chisel site nicely illustrates the atmosphere:

I arrive at Chisel. As usual the car park is full of cars. Outside the entrance, there is a Swedish flag and birch twigs with blue and yellow balloons and garlands. Five or six students, in light summer clothes, are standing next to the entrance, smoking ... We say 'Hi' to each other and I go upstairs, down the corridor to the canteen. I have been invited to the last lunch of the school year. The tables are laid with white tablecloths. Blue cornflowers, yellow roses, blue and yellow garlands, decorate the tables. The canteen is crowded with students, teachers, instructors and invited staff, such as the headmaster, career adviser, school curator, etc. Everybody looks happy and there is a cheerful atmosphere. After lunch, consisting of an enormous Swedish 'smorgasbord' and strawberry cake, the headmaster and some of the teachers make short speeches and various kinds of diplomas are distributed to the students. The students look really happy and in some cases even a little embarrassed, yet pleased, when they receive their diplomas. The thought strikes me that this is perhaps the first time many of these students have attracted attention in positive school circumstances. I hear utterances such as: 'Oh, I couldn't even dream of this (to get a diploma)', or, 'I can't believe it'. I felt truly touched at that

moment. Happy looking students give the staff hugs; some quite reserved
others genuine and heartfelt. Even I got a lot of them before they leave
the room for a new summer holiday.   (Field notes Chisel, June 2009)

The good atmosphere was built on an orientation towards the emotional.
The pedagogic code had a strong focus on building personal relations with
'disadvantaged and low achieving students' as the headmaster expressed it. Given
that, it seemed natural to focus on a slow pace and good mood, well-being and
comfort, rather than on high quality education. The emphasis on maintaining a
'good mood' was also promoted by the fact that the Individual Programme was
considered as 'the loser's programme' (Julia, student), a notion that was reflected
in comments by both staff and students (see also Hultqvist, 2001; Johansson,
2009). Stig (teacher) strongly expressed how people in the surroundings like
colleagues, in both secondary and upper secondary schools, apprehended the
group of students on the programme, as 'weak' and 'a bit odd' and he stressed
the importance of being keenly sensitive with 'this group of students':

> Many of these students have a tough time ... and it's very important
> that *somebody* likes them ... who work with this type of student. Many
> of them have lost their faith in adults and it's all about recreating that
> [faith] again ... it's very important.   (Interview Stig, May 2009)

Such a comment corroborates the assumption that the Individual Programme
hosts a 'special group of students' with individual deficits and inner problems. The
headmaster confirmed that teachers and students expressed feelings that they
were 'outside the system' and many students articulated feelings of exclusion in
comments such as, 'We are all stupid ... that is why we are on the IP [Individual
Programme]'; 'We are all mongoloids [have Down's Syndrome]'.

Sometimes this exclusion was expressed in heartbreaking treatments. One
example was provided by Caroline, who told me that she really missed her old
friend a lot and went on: 'We were always together, we live next door ... but
... you know ... social science [students] don't associate with IPs [Individual
Programme students]'. Stine, the (substitute) teacher heard the conversation and
looked puzzled at the girl asking: 'Do you call yourselves IPs?' Both Caroline
and Mary, who were sitting next to her, shouted in chorus: 'THEY [all the other
students and teachers] call us IPs!'

The notion of low status made teachers 'feel sorry' (Inez) for students and prioritised the interpersonal relations (see also Hugo, 2007) over goal achievement. The fact that only forty-five per cent of the students who attended the Individual Programme at Currant Upper passed their subjects so they could attend a National Programme after one year illustrates this. Hence, there was a profound risk of the students ending up outside both education and work after finishing school (Olofsson and Wadensjö, 2007). There is an increasing gap between over- and under-achievers, which has a clear relationship with students' socio-economic backgrounds.

According to Hugo (2007), the interpersonal relationships between students and teachers are crucial; it seems to be important to pay attention to factors beyond studies and goal effectiveness in order for students to thrive. The teachers observed in his study had to play diverse roles (social worker, parent etc.), far from solely as an 'educator', that muddled profession and personality. To be a 'caring person' you have to incorporate personal traits like 'kindness,' 'loving' and 'thoughtfulness' (Skeggs, 1997). Stig, like a great majority of the staff, focused on the private and emotional rather than on knowledge, future studies and work. However, Lemar (2001) suggests that this poses risks of setting a 'care trap'. Some teachers' roles at upper secondary school will only embrace students in difficulty (see also chapter five). They are supposed to, and do, focus on care when meeting different students, but this is not valued in an academically and theoretically oriented knowledge culture, and they will thus acquire low status in upper secondary school. Students and teachers on the Individual Programme will not only have low status in others' eyes, but also their own, compared to students and teachers of National Programmes.

Experiences of formal influence

In the previous sections, some characteristics of the Individual Programme have been outlined and discussed, including: the seemingly rich opportunities for students to influence their teaching, students' choice of the easiest solution in this situation, and most teachers' focus on private and emotional aspects rather than on academic performance. A key issue that remains to be explored is what possibilities were available to the students to 'act citizenship' in this context (Gordon, 2006).

According to the Swedish curriculum, Lpf 94, upper secondary school has a three-fold democracy mission: to develop the students' democratic knowledge and skills, to do so through democratic working forms, and to mediate democratic values (Ministry of Education and Research, 1994, see also chapter two). Democratic competence is seen as something that young people should develop both within and outside the walls of school. In this respect, the school is regarded as a key institution that should play a central role in the students' acquisition of democratic skills, and thus provide important foundations for the future society (Swedish National Agency for Education, 2010a). This raises questions about whether everyday practice in the studied Individual Programme fostered the desired democratic skills, and if so in what ways? What opportunities and possibilities to 'act citizenship' (Gordon, 2006) were observed? We will now take a closer look at the formal structures such as class and student councils.

Formal structures, such as class and student councils, might provide important arenas that allow students to initiate acts of influence (Öhrn, 1998, 2001). Every 'home group' of Quill students had one lesson a week reserved for a class council lesson. During this lesson, questions concerning everyday life were mostly raised, such as how the students got on at school and when an excursion was to be planned, or alternatively the time was simply used as an opportunity to do exercises intended to 'form a group' out of 'all these solitaries' as Stine put it or 'just gather over a cup of coffee' (Ruth). According to my field notes it was never used as formal meeting time as a traditional class council lesson with a chairperson, secretary and written minutes.

In the Chisel section there were no class councils, but a 'consultation group' (Inez), consisting of both teachers and students. According to Inez, the aim of the group was to 'discuss both the organisation and content' of the everyday school work. One female and one male student were appointed at the beginning of the school year to represent the group of students. However, there were no formal meetings during the time of the fieldwork and even though teachers talked about 'the importance and value of (and need for) the group' (Inez), in practice it seemed to have little significance, and there was very little interest or involvement of the students. When both students representatives became ill in the middle of the autumn semester, and did not return to school during the rest of the school year, nobody else was chosen to represent the Chisel students, even though voting for new representatives was on the agenda several times. Furthermore, although teachers talked about the importance of students' councils and consultation groups, they did not take any steps to make them work and they never became a normal part of everyday school life:

Today I went to Chisel to observe the voting for new representatives to the consultation group, which was promised last Friday. After the lesson Inez realised that it had been forgotten again: 'Oh ... now we forgot the voting ... it [the lesson] was so messy ... we can do it after the break'. There was no voting after the break either.

(Field notes Chisel, November 2008)

Öhrn (1998, 2005) points out the importance of students acquiring knowledge about and being involved in formal democratic structures so that they may become better able to influence everyday school life. She notes that students consider that the time spent on class and students' councils provides opportunities to raise issues, but at the same time they are generally sceptical about the importance of the councils. In addition, according to Almgren (2006, p. 167), young people who are directly involved in class and student councils acquire more political self confidence than others, which in turn further promotes their desire to participate in other political actions.

To summarise, there were no traditional formal structures of student influence and impact at the group/class level in the studied Individual Programme, even though both Chisel and Quill teachers talked about the importance of such arenas. At Current Upper there was a working student council. According to minutes, a broad range of issues, ranging from withdrawn courses and supervision cameras, through uncomfortable chairs and arrangements for school balls, to the quality of toilet paper and the layout of the photo catalogue were on the agenda. These issues concern students' daily life. At Currant Upper every class was supposed to be represented in the council, but no students represented the students (more than one hundred and twenty) of the Individual Programme. According to both Quill and Chisel teachers, the students 'didn't want to go to the main building' (Vera) where meetings were held. However, in reality they did not 'feel welcome', Lars, one of the teachers, pointed out. Lydia, another teacher, told me about the problem:

Every programme or class is supposed to send one representative ...
[There are no Individual Programme representatives] but that really
... is a typical example of the fact that our students aren't interlinked ...
nobody wants to go down [to the main building] ... they don't even want
to go down to the canteen ...   (Field notes Quill, September 2008)

Moreover, the distance to the main building, at least from Chisel, made it almost impossible for the students to attend the student council's meetings. However, it was not an issue students emphasised; on the contrary, during interviews and fieldwork students expressed doubt about the value of councils. Many of them even said that it did not concern them. During the interviews, when I asked them about their experience of these forums during compulsory school, all but three of the twenty-four interviewed students talked about it in terms of 'it did not concern' them or it was 'not their business'. A majority of them had never been involved as chairpersons or secretaries during their nine years in compulsory school.

To be a chairperson or secretary was obviously not something you had to try during compulsory school. On the contrary, several of the students testified that 'you had to apply for it' (Rina) and then there was 'voting among the school mates' (John). It was 'always the same persons', Rina told me. If students had experiences at all, they were mostly negative, as Jim and Tobias revealed during a social sciences lesson:

> Jim asks the teacher, by the way: 'Why do you have student council? Honestly … why?' The teacher looks at him and is just going to answer him when Tobias interrupts and turns to Jim: 'If you want a new football court … that is supposed to be decided by the student council … and then … the headmaster makes a decision that we can't have it'. The students make a lot of jokes about their experiences of students' councils while the teacher makes strenuous efforts to defend the role of the council due to its importance for raising questions about power [bullying, gender issues, racism etc.].   (Field notes Quill, April 2009)

The excerpt above illustrates one of very few occasions when the power of the students' council, and students' power in relation to the school's formal decision-making structure in general, was discussed. Issues related to education were rather handled exclusively between teacher and student. In other words, the degree of potential impact was dependent in practice on the individual student and teacher, rather than on formal structures. In this manner the democratic mandate was left to the individual teacher to cope with and student influence became mainly informal influence linked to every individual person (see also Dovemark 2004a, 2008). Willy, the social sciences teacher, expressed frustration with this system. He said it was problematic when it was not formalised:

It's up to each teacher to act or not ... it's not fair. The students don't learn how to act in a democracy. We really should have a working students' council ... but we haven't. Now it's more up to each teacher or the headmaster. The students' council really should be given more space, it's important.

Willy went on to emphasise the importance of learning democratic skills as a way to 'learn to consider others' opinions, not only your own, and 'that you can't get everything you want'. He pointed out: 'To suffer defeat is also part of democracy'. He expressed worry about the informalised practice and stated that 'learning democracy' should be more integrated in the structure of the school: 'It really should be the norm, we the teachers really should accept, and even expect, the students to raise issues and fight for their rights'. Willy seemed to be very clear about how to engage and encourage young people to make their voices heard. The problem, he stated, was the students' lack of familiarity with 'taking steps to make it work'. Willy, and several of his colleagues, emphasised the problem of students not being 'educated in democracy'. It 'shouldn't be something you can choose or not, but a natural part of all education', he said, and noted the contradiction between the emphasis on 'freedom of choice' and lack of learning about democracy in practice on the Individual Programme.

To summarise, there were no representatives from the Individual Programme in any formal forum at Currant Upper, except for two students in a group working against bullying. In practice, students of the Individual programme were excluded from the students' council and representative influence generally, and were effectively marginalised at Currant Upper. Teachers talked about the importance of the students' council and consultation groups, but they never took any steps to make them work and they never became a normal part of everyday school life. Acting citizenship requires individuals to believe in their own capacity and acquire the necessary knowledge to form standpoints and make decisions, in other words democratic competence to pursue political activities (Ekman, 2007). Formal structures of student influence in the studied Individual Programme were non-existent, or at best non-functional, according to both observations and interviews. The next section takes a closer look at that issue.

Democratic competence

In a teaching practice where textbooks provided the structuring principles, general questions about the world, social life and challenges to the perception of subordination were seldom raised. This was a thing that struck me during the fieldwork. I seldom observed students taking the initiative to change to a more context-independent pedagogic structure (or ask for such a change), or heard them complain about poor premises like rundown locations, the distance to the cafeterias and library, lack of sports facilities etc. Compared to students of the national programmes, who were situated in recently refurbished school buildings and classrooms with new, brightly coloured furniture, they seemed to come off worst, but put up with it. When talking to teachers about students' attempts to influence things, with few exceptions, they confirmed these observations. Stine was one of them; when I asked her about the students' determination, capacity and power to exert influence to change their work or working environment, she like many of her colleagues, expressed doubt:

> No, no, no … they never show any interest in that … we have to push them … *If* they make a proposal to do something else … it's always a proposal like … to watch a film or play a game … something like that … it's always proposals to 'lay back', hang around even more … in other words to avoid doing anything.   (Field notes Quill, November 2008)

According to Stine, students' influence concerned counter-productive things, to avoid work (see also Dovemark, 2004a, 2004b, 2007, 2008) rather than raising questions about content, practice and the social world. Stine found a lack of students' initiative for change and influence, which she occasionally tried to stimulate through different school tasks like writing in to the local newspaper. She continued:

> I often try to put it [how to make an impact] on the agenda. One example is related to the occasions when I try to persuade them to send letters to the newspaper. I have never met so many … where all of them say things like 'but I haven't any opinions about those things … so I haven't anything to write', if I create a task to write a letter. I try to ask 'What is your opinion … that is what do you think about something' and then they say, 'but I still don't think anything' and then, 'well, then I don't need to do anything'. I feel really worried … or it really feels hard … many things … I experience that they don't feel involved in … or take initiative to be involved … many of them withdraw [into themselves] and

start to chat [on the net], surf and send text messages and mess around.
(Field notes Quill, November 2008)

Stine went on to explain that the 'absence of willingness to make an impact' was not just about 'big things like the EU election' (which was going on during the fieldwork), but also about minor things in everyday life, such as 'small school matters'. She told me that the students did not seem to be 'trained in argumentation' and if they did they had 'very thin arguments' and they 'just dismissed it; this is shit, this sucks' and 'always turned their attention away from any ideas that they may have had'. The level of political self-confidence seemed to be low and Stine expressed doubt about the feasibility of compensating the students for not acquiring democratic skills and knowledge in secondary school (see also chapter five). Ekman's (2007) study of vocational programmes in Swedish upper secondary school confirms the difficulties of compensating for missing democratic skills and knowledge.

To summarise, although possibilities were there, the students seemed to accept the presented organisation and the strongly classified content. They were not 'used to or trained in democracy' Stine pointed out. According to Ekman (2007, p. 163) there are differences in democratic skills among upper secondary school programmes, since students on the academic programmes are offered a more democratic learning environment than those on vocational programmes. Hence, the differences in democratic competence between students attending academic and vocational programmes will probably increase during their years in upper secondary school.

My study indicates that the Individual Programme is likely to put students at a similar disadvantage to those on vocational programmes, since textbooks provide structuring principles of specific examinable content while other aspects of knowledge, such as reflection, calculation and analysis, are to a great extent excluded. Hence, schools seem to accept and normalise a perception of subordination and exclusion of students on programmes like the Individual Programme, in the way they are organised, i.e. through streamed education and material. Teaching and learning are thus regarded as simply a process of technical transmission of an already organised subject, rather than preparing young people for broader purposes such as participation in a democratic society (Englund, 2004). Issues and problems of everyday life are pushed into the background as part of the educational process.

Due to the students' lack of practicing influence there was a risk of preparing them for roles in the margins of society outside education and work (Olofsson and Wadensjö, 2007), as second-class citizens (the Swedish National Board of Youth Affairs, 2008). So, even though superficially everybody may seem to have the same rights in today's neo-liberal school system, there surely are educational and social inequalities. However, the picture is not complete. Even though the organisation and teaching had a strong emphasis on the individual nature of citizenship (Gordon, 2006), stressing autonomy and individualisation rather than collective actions, there were strong exceptions when students took initiative and were encouraged by teachers to act as citizens (see Dovemark, 2010).

For instance, during the year of fieldwork some girls showed great concern about the continuous sexual harassment many girls endured during their school days. Although they talked to the staff about this issue, and appealed several times for them to be present more often during lecture-free time, nothing really happened. They then took the initiative to act in favour of a friend on a National Programme who had been the victim of a public humiliation campaign. They tried to start discussion groups on 'how to treat each other', made posters and put up posters in various locations in the main building, with messages such as: 'Do you realise how bad you feel when people are talking bullshit about you? Do you know how it feels to be outcast?' They acted with both force and energy to make a change. Eric was another student who, after talking to the Social Sciences teacher, started an action to save the café at the Quill site. The café had been opened, closed down and reopened several times. When I started the fieldwork in the autumn of 2008 the café was closed. Both students and staff regarded the café as an important issue to pursue.

Eric's proposal resulted in an action in which he and some friends, with support from teachers, decided to make a petition, pleaded with students at Currant Upper to sign it and handed it to the headmaster. The next example includes political actions outside school. A demonstration organised by the Swedish National Democrats (a right-wing populist party) was held at the market place in Lake City. News about the demonstration spread rapidly throughout school, particularly among the immigrants. Many of them were upset, and the social sciences teacher took the opportunity to tell the students about the party and its policy. According to him it resulted in an action by several of them, primarily the immigrant youth. They 'simply marched down to the market' and 'posed questions' to the representatives of the Swedish National Democrats. They questioned the party's immigration policy and tried to get answers about their own refugee status. The social sciences teacher explained to me with emphasis: 'Young people really are active, maybe not organised in the way we used to think, but active when they get support and we promote collective actions'. The value of committed adults and the importance of adults supporting and promoting young people's attempts to react to events and policies they object to, and support those that they favour, are also stressed by other researchers (see, for instance, Ekman, 2007; Johansson, 2007; Öhrn, 2009).

Conclusions

The students of the studied Individual Programme were strongly isolated from students taking the national programmes, and the rest of the school, in terms of locations, staff and the possibilities to exercise influence formally through the students' council. A strong subordination was identified. However, in some respects the most germane result of the study is the prevailing construction of the students as needy, low-achieving students 'with special needs' (Lars, teacher). Relations of the staff with the students were focused on private emotional facets, rather than on providing high quality education with high achievements (see also chapter five). Thus, even though students had high ambitions at the beginning of the school year, the pace of their learning, and ambitions, soon fell (see also chapters five and seven; Hjelmér et al. 2010). In this way they acquired a lowly status in the classification system of the Upper secondary school, and in society as a whole (Bernstein, 2000).

In this fragmentised, individual and private environment there were few recorded attempts by students to influence the organisation and content of their education, besides an informal, strongly counter-productive freedom of choice, which mainly resulted in reductions in pace and course items. In this manner, the students acquired a legitimate pedagogic code within the Individual Programme, with its focus on the private, personal and emotional. However, it was not a code that the academically-oriented upper secondary school valued. Hence the Individual Programme acquired a low status.

The empirical data suggest that the studied programme had potential to promote democracy that was not exploited. Although some teachers, particularly social sciences teachers encouraged students' activities, and teachers generally expressed the importance of democratic education, it was not orchestrated. Furthermore, the students on the Individual Programme at Currant Upper were not compensated for their lack of acquisition of democratic skills and knowledge from secondary school (see also chapter five). To the contrary, their social disadvantages seemed to be reproduced and reinforced in new ways. In today's neo-liberal economy students are forced to 'choose' their subordination through so-called 'freedom of choice' (Dovemark, 2004a, 2004b, 2008), which for the Individual Programme students, proved to be counter-productive, differentiating and even more isolating. A majority (fifty-five per cent) of the students ended up in the margins of the school and did not attain the stated goal for the programme, eligibility for a national programme; and those who do not complete upper secondary education have increased risks of unemployment or doing various part-time, insecure and temporary service jobs after leaving school (see also Olofsson and Wadensjö, 2007).

Teachers of the studied Individual Programme seemed to pay little attention to teaching the students the code of a high achieving student, and the right attitude to study (the instructional discourse), i.e. hard work. A key problem was that the students were not really taught about the regulative discourse, i.e. what resources should be used to talk to teachers to exercise influence. Both teaching and fostering democratic citizens seemed to be neglected, or at least far down on the staff's priorities, and far from the official ideology of creating a 'school for all' with equal chances and possibilities.

Chapter 9

Synthesis

Dennis Beach, Lisbeth Lundahl and Elisabet Öhrn

In this final chapter we attempt to synthesise the research issues and findings regarding democratic education and student influence. We start by drawing together results on central themes from the five previous empirical chapters by Carina Hjelmér (chapters four and five), Per-Åke Rosvall (chapters six and seven) and Marianne Dovemark (chapter eight). The central themes are as follows; teaching students to influence; student initiatives to exert influence; conditions for developing valued masculinities and femininities; the reproduction of hierarchical relations; and representations and relations of theory and practice.

Teaching students to influence

The analyses of the various programmes and study groups show few instances of formalised teaching about how students can exercise influence in school, such teaching rather concerns the principles of representative democracy and its procedures and representations in various countries and the EU. This focus coincides with that of Swedish textbooks (Bronäs, 2008), and means that forms of influence typically used by youth without voting rights are seldom addressed in class. Furthermore, the kind of representative democracy that is usually present in schools in the form of student councils appears to attract little student interest and to have little effect on school decisions.

It is well known that formal school organisations are not powerful means for students to exert influence, and that students might be disciplined and supervised through what appear to be participatory processes (Davies, 2002). However, this is not to say that there is no democratic value in organisations such as school councils. As shown in Öhrn (1998), the councils can provide significant *opportunities* to communicate with teachers and potential spaces for criticism that students might choose to use without fighting their way to negotiations. In addition, they may help the development of certain formal democratic techniques and competences, as shown by Rönnlund (2010) in an analysis of students' action groups that were organised in accordance with student councils' routines and models. This is a kind of organisation that is familiar to Swedish youth from compulsory school, but according to our studies it does not seem to be developed further at the upper secondary level.

The lack of regular formalised teaching about influence does not mean that the students in the studied classes were left without guidance. Both assistance and direct teaching were provided in instances when students themselves had already initiated targeted action. This was manifested on various occasions, for instance when the students in the Natural Science class (chapter four) tried to influence the pace and content of their maths teaching and obtained teacher instructions on how to act. It also emerged when the students of the Vehicle Programme (chapter seven) reacted against the lack of substitute maths teachers. A teacher set out to teach them how to organise their protest, by emphasising the importance of collective action and the advantages of formal meeting protocols to back up requests. The teacher also taught them techniques required to pursue these activities effectively. It should be noted that throughout the various cases the supported techniques rested on negotiations. There was no encouragement or aid to mount more confrontational actions, as teachers have sometimes been seen to provide when students target organisations or policies outside school (Öhrn, 2004, 2005).

In all probability, the Vehicle Programme teacher's experience of trade union work outside school helped enable him to teach the students about practical strategies of influence. More generally, teachers' *lack* of experience of such work and collective actions in places of work is presumably one of the reasons why they are commonly passive and ill-equipped for teaching students about, and promoting, democratic structures in school.

That the students were offered aid after instigating processes of influence might be interpreted as an indication of responsiveness from teachers to the specific needs of individual groups. However, an alternative interpretation is that getting access to this kind of teaching presupposes student initiative, which is in line with students' views that they themselves are responsible for exerting influence in school. The exclusivity of this access is further emphasised by the fact that teaching in the researched classes was largely individualised. This was particularly pronounced at the Individual Programme where so few common educational activities took place that it was often difficult even to speak of the existence of classes or groups over time. Instead, students generally worked in small groups or individually, so the classroom was not a shared public arena for the exchange of knowledge. Consequently, a silent audience could not learn from the discussions and strategies of others, as is generally the case in public teacher-centred education (cf. Österlind, 1998). In this manner, the individualised practice may reduce the chances of joint student criticism and group formation in class.

While students in most of the observed classes were invited to influence administrative aspects of teaching, such as the order of studying a certain content, timing of tests and presentations—that is the framing of educational communication, but not the classification of content—their options for voicing criticism and suggesting changes varied according to context. Above all, they differed according to the status of the various subjects, programmes and groups of students. For instance, the subjects and programmes that were the most amenable to student influence were the least prestigious. This aspect is discussed at greater length below.

Student initiatives to exert influence

Several basic questions have guided our attempts to address, describe and analyse the ways students have influenced (or tried to influence) issues at school. One important question has been whether the students can change anything or not, and if so, what they can affect and in what kind of contexts. Another important question has been whether students act collectively or individually, and how the schools and the teachers respond. Although a collective approach has not been adopted in most cases, we have observed some examples of students collectively acting to influence the pace and support in mathematics and computer studies (chapters four and five). More often, however, collective actions are about non-teaching matters, e.g. access to facilities (chapters seven and eight), and resisting harassment and racism (chapter eight). With the exception of the computer studies case (chapter five), the collective actions have resulted in at most marginal changes.

Context is important. As suggested in Beach (2008), different spaces for creative influence and self-realisation are socially constructed, and subjectively understood and valued in schools by students. Comparisons between teaching and learning practices and experiences in different subjects suggest that the presence of strong currents of performativity have profound implications for whether students want influence, what they want to influence and how they are prepared and willing to act in order to do so. In academic subjects students generally favoured the use of strong forms of external control and visible pedagogy by teachers that led to an uncomplicated delivery of 'right answers' and what students felt was correct knowledge, particularly if this knowledge was expected to crop up in any formal examination or grading context.

This kind of situation also seems to fit the academic programmes and subject contexts of the present study. With few exceptions there was little attempt to influence formal contents in these programmes and subjects, except when the pace was felt to be so fast that it was impossible to keep up, as in the maths lessons of the Natural Science class. In the Social Science class, for instance, students were not offered any opportunity, and took no initiative, to influence the contents, although they contended that there were things they were not comfortable with and would like to change. Indeed, it seems that although they were not completely happy with the situation, like the science students, they accepted things pretty much as there was 'clarity of instruction', 'good attention to detail', 'a high level of positive control', 'clear boundary maintenance', 'clear descriptions of assessment criteria', and 'openness and fairness in grading and assessment'. Again, this strongly accords with previous findings reported by Beach (2008).

The attempts to influence the teaching of mathematics by the Natural Science class, and the final outcome of those attempts, are quite significant here. These students tried to influence the pace, level of difficulty, choice of textbook and grading in mathematics, and they clearly did so collectively, but without success. Employing individualising technologies, the staff quickly closed ranks by basically saying that the subject was not amenable in this programme, at the level of study in question, to the requested reduction of pace and dilution of content. In fact, they added, the problem did not lie in the way mathematics was taught, or the quality of the illustrative materials used, but in the individual learning difficulties of some students (see also Beach, 1999a). In short, the underlying causes of the problems collectively identified by the students were transformed from teaching-related factors to individuals' deficiencies.

In the Vehicle class, repeated cancellations of mathematics lessons due to the teacher's illness led to protests from the students. No compensatory measures were taken, however, and when students' absenteeism rose in maths lessons, the situation was primarily explained in terms of students' lack of interest. The two cases are similar in that the difficulties were attributed, by the school, to shortcomings of the students rather than the teacher or school. However, in the case of the Natural Science class, the proposals of the students were rejected with the argument that it was impossible to lower the standards of teaching, while in the Vehicle class (and computer studies in the Child and Recreation class) the school accepted that students did not get the teaching they were entitled to.

The responses of the students attending academic programmes are also worth considering here. These students generally seemed skilled in assessing whether it was worthwhile to pursue an issue, and they stopped actions when they realised that they were not likely to achieve any changes. In addition, they were likely to express that their own personal learning problems in the subjects may be creating their difficulties and that they needed to increase their efforts and buck their ideas up.

A further factor that contributed to the ways in which the Natural Science students planned actions and moderated their behaviour were the perceived effects on their marks (cf. Öhrn, 1998; Beach, 2008; Beach and Dovemark, 2007). Concern about educational success seemed to be implicated not only in terms of high marks and test performance, but also in showing appropriate behaviour. Making the right choices and showing an interest and willingness to work or to present interest compatible with expectations of talent may be no less important than academic performance (see also Beach and Dovemark, 2009). Such expectations are, however, classed and gendered, and girls' genuine interest and/or talent, especially, appear to be ambivalent and even controversial issues in school (Lahelma and Öhrn, 2003).

Concerns about marks and other forms of study achievement seemed to be weaker driving forces of the strategies and actions, or lack of them, in the two vocational classes and the Individual Programme. When students in the Child and Recreation class raised critique against the computer studies teacher, they thus appeared less concerned about study success or failure, but were upset by the teacher being unfriendly and demanding.

In the Vehicle class, the perceptions of study success often seemed to be clearly associated with the requirements of the vehicle mechanic occupation—practical skills and discipline as well as competence in Swedish and English, in order (for instance) to be able to read manuals. Students' protests about cancelled maths lessons may be understood in this light; mathematics was perceived to be important both in work as a vehicle mechanic and for further vocational studies, which some of the students were aiming to pursue. In the highly individualised and fragmented study situation of the Individual Programme, students' actions did not concern teaching matters. Here, as well as in the Child and Recreation class, lack of health and well-being were more prominent factors behind dissatisfaction and efforts to exert influence than teaching contents. The lack of a clear occupational orientation of the Child and Recreation Programme and the Individual Programme (unless related to a vocational programme) may have contributed to this.

In the two vocational classes and the Individual Programme there were examples of both individual and collective efforts to change perceived inconveniences, but these were mostly actions conducted individually or in small groups. In the Vehicle Programme, the class council was used to try to exert influence over mathematics teaching. However, there is not much information about the collective versus individual action dimension. The Child and Recreation Programme students' efforts to jointly influence the teaching in computer studies was initially a 'collective move', but the action had barely started before the adults took over and assumed responsibility for it. Other examples of influence in this class were the almost daily negotiations initiated by these students to reduce the length of lessons by adding extra breaks or extending scheduled breaks. These efforts were often based on individual initiatives that then received support from a small but vociferous group, even though the outcome usually applied to everyone in the class.

Conditions for developing valued masculinities and femininities

Gendered practices were present within each programme, but were especially visible in differences between the predominantly female Child and Recreation Programme and the predominantly male Vehicle Programme. As explored by Hjelmér, Lappalainen and Rosvall (2010), the various gendered practices include the Vehicle Programme being organised in a way that simulated working life, whereas the Child and Recreation Programme was organised through a time-table associated with the school.

The Vehicle Programme prepares students for a clearly identified career, or set of careers, and this constituted the basis for a work-related content and daily production-related routines. Far more diffuse in terms of vocational choices and careers, the Child and Recreation Programme really appears to be non-theoretical rather than vocational. This programme can, potentially, lead to further education in vocational university-based nursery and infant or leisure education studies.

What we see then, are vocational programmes that differ significantly with respect to relations to the labour market and merits for future life. Our study included just two vocational programmes, but such differences could be said to apply to the majority of such programmes. Formal Swedish and

Scandinavian schooling is organised so that programmes leading to traditional male occupations are located at the upper-secondary instead of university level more often than traditional female occupations. Consequently, young working class males can avoid university studies, without substantially jeopardising their chances of valued employment, through the availability of direct connections between typically male programmes such as the Construction and Vehicle programmes.

Programmes with this kind of direct connectivity are not available to young working class women (or are at least not recognised by them as available or grasped by them) to the same extent (see Arnesen, Lahelma and Öhrn, 2008). Furthermore, in school this seems to mean that there is a rather distinct, locally highly valued masculinity associated with the Vehicle Programme and similar programmes with direct connections to economic production that may entice young males into these lines of work (cf. Willis, 1977).

A similarly clear positive femininity is difficult to discern in the Child and Recreation Programme, which instead leads to low-paid socialised labour. In addition, as further explored below, the lack of distinct programme identity appears to be related to students not identifying and explicitly requesting competences needed for their future careers from the school. However, many students in the Child and Recreation class expressed disappointment when they realised that the curriculum included little of the contents they had expected relating to children and child development.

The masculine ideals expressed by the boys in the Vehicle Programme clearly relate to a well-known working-class masculinity (Willis, 1977, 2004; Pattman, Frosh and Phoenix, 2005). This manifests in the boys' celebration of manual labour and their disapproval of the 'girly' parts of the programme and associated aspects. However, some of their responses related to theoretical studies indicate possible challenges to these ideals, emanating from the recognised links between academic qualifications and good pay, good working conditions and advancement. In this respect, the boys may draw on key demands of traditional working-class masculinities and struggle—including economic compensation and control of working conditions—to elaborate on issues of masculinity to include more pro-education aspects.

This might be taken to conflict with the presentation of working-class boys as generally opposed to education (cf. Dolby, Dimitriadis and Willis, 2004). Statistics showing that school achievement varies significantly between areas with similar socio-economic structure adds further contradiction (Swedish National

Agency for Education, 2009b). These things might suggest, we would argue, that emerging working-class masculinities are less dismissive of education and more open to adaptation to changes in the labour market than often assumed. This is also discussed in chapter one.

The reproduction of hierarchical relations

A hierarchy among programmes is evident in descriptions by both students and teachers. It can also be seen in differences between programmes in the physical environment, including the closeness (and newness) of buildings housing them to the centre of the school and proximity to activities (see also Johansson, 2009). The location of student council meetings at the schools provides an example; they were usually situated closer to the academic students, who appeared to be expected to take part more often in such activities, than the vocational students. In one of the schools, the school information screens were also centrally placed in the main hallway of the school's main building, which was not normally used by vocational students as their activities were based in separate buildings.

Such indications of status differences seem to carry over into, and affect, student experiences, emotions and feelings. As the Individual Programme students regularly pointed out, they felt that they were at the margins of the school and regularly described themselves as less able and/or less interested in obtaining high marks than other students, and of being belittled by teachers and other people. Comments about ritualism, recalcitrance and an absence of a clear sense of the purpose of school were also common (e.g. Woods, 1979; Ball, 1981; Hamilton, 1989; Dovemark, 2004a).

We can bring these two lines of reasoning and their empirical basis together; whilst academically oriented students are often physically, subjectively and even emotionally placed at the centre of the school and are talked about by teachers (and themselves) as being in school to obtain good marks in important subjects that can be exchanged for a good education and a good job or career in the future, the students of some of the vocational and (even more so) the individual programmes are placed outside the centre and are often talked about as being less interested, less involved, less committed and less bright.

A pattern emerges when we look across the five studied groups in relation to the hierarchy discussed above, which is also reflected in the dimensions of power students are given with respect to their degree of influence in the subjects and programmes. The subjects and programmes that are positioned as less prestigious seem to be more open to influence than the more high status subjects and programmes. This applies especially to mathematics, which is portrayed in the researched classes as almost naturally given. Henderson and Hudson (2010) similarly speak of a mathematics content that is unshakable and extremely difficult to influence by either the students or the teachers. They describe the workings of a kind of mathematics fundamentalism, which we can also trace in our study.

Using concepts proposed by Bernstein we can analyse the influence of two different kinds of subject content discourse: horizontal and vertical. These two discourses are very different from each other. A vertical discourse is developed from the integration of expressions of meaning in a particular specialised field or area to form a coherent, systematically principled and explicit conceptual structure with a robust grammar and specialised syntax that is hierarchically organised and expressed through a highly esoteric language (Bernstein, 2000, pp. 170-171).

This structure of discourse is usually called a discipline. It is characteristic of academic subjects like physics, mathematics and history, and when constructing curricula and courses in such subjects, schools and universities usually select content for instruction from these fields of production and thereby act as re-contextualising arenas for the knowledge produced therein. This knowledge is then sequentially ordered in a curriculum according to a logic of transmission that is oriented toward the production of highly specialised texts and practices (Bernstein, 2000) that are strongly embedded in particular social and institutional sites and very difficult to influence from the outside (Beach and Bagley, 2010). This may explain why it is accepted that there is little possibility for students to influence the content in these subjects in school. Examination practices and the rules of evaluation in these areas add to this limitation.

Horizontal discourses are very different. They are formed and based on knowledge that is local and tied to a specific practical context. They are therefore less formally assured and 'powerful' than scientific knowledge of the above kind in institutions such as schools that use subject knowledge to mark and evaluate performances, in that they are less systematically formed and lack an anchoring dimension of specialised inquiry and systematic public evaluation controlled by a professional hierarchy based on a socially (academically) proven and politically legitimated expertise. This, Bernstein adds, is also significant in other senses, as these absences may mean that the knowledge interests of the education can be more easily manoeuvred and influenced from the outside. Vocational knowledge is generally constructed and distributed outside of, and even independently of, disciplinary hierarchies as pedagogic re-contextualising fields. Here the vocation itself is more influential, and in Sweden this will probably become even more accentuated when the 2009 upper secondary school reform is implemented in 2011.

The analysis of young people's influence in the empirical chapters fits this line of reasoning, as it shows how the hierarchy between subjects represents relationships not only between subjects but also, and more importantly, between fields of practice (vocational and academic). The more academic the subject content the more status the subject has in school in terms of resilience to external (horizontal) influence and the less academic the less the resilience. This applies we would say even to the extent that responsibility for formulating, aggregating and communicating key forms of knowledge can be placed elsewhere and outside the direct control of academic agents like school teachers.

Thus, what is clearest in relation to mathematics in the Natural Science class, where students failed to affect teaching content or its relations of reproduction and re-contextualisation, reflects a particular logic. The observation that the Social Science class did not even try to affect their mathematics education corroborates this, and confirms our assumptions. But the relationship is not just about subject content, it also reflects (and reinforces) divisions of labour, social class, social fields and class power (Beach, 2005). Two further interesting points here are: first, that the pattern of the students' desires to avoid instruction in the Vehicle Programme is heeded more than their demands for deeper subject matter and a more demanding academic education; and second, that students of the vocational programmes have most scope for influencing their education, but largely in terms of diluting academic demands and avoiding lessons and teaching.

Representations and relations of theory and practice

The scope of core subjects such as Swedish, English, mathematics and history in vocational education and training has been a recurrent, controversial issue in Swedish education politics (Lundahl, 1997; Lundahl, Erixon Arreman, Lundström and Rönnberg, 2010). The 2009 upper secondary education reform will, *inter alia*, lead to a reallocation of teaching time: a reduction of the time allotted to academic subjects in vocational education and training, and conversely more space for vocational subjects. Knowledge will be more strongly classified, i.e. the boundaries between different subjects and teacher categories will be sharper again. For example, the contents of core subjects are to be adjusted in line with the main orientation of the vocational programmes (e.g. 'industrial Swedish' will be taught in the Industry Programme). The change is mainly motivated by an alleged need to focus on vocational preparation and employability, and more or less explicit assumptions that vocational students have less need for general courses in e.g. Swedish, mathematics and English (Lundahl et al., 2010).

Our research allows us to question such assumptions about accepted differences between academic and vocational students, not least assumptions about the lack of theoretical interest amongst those who choose vocational programmes, for several reasons. Firstly, there is little evidence that what goes on in classrooms has anything to do with essential traits of these students. On the contrary, the assumptions seem to be as often refuted as confirmed by student actions and the orthodox conclusions thus seem to rest entirely on foundations that are socially constructed elements of a dominant discourse about social belonging, social origins, labour and intellectual ability (Beach, 2005). Secondly, the class and gender aspects and the relationships of power and relative autonomy of the academic and vocational fields must also be taken into consideration. These have, we suggest, more explanatory power than other factors regarding the differences noted and registered at the empirical level. Indeed, overall the studies show that there is no distinction between students of vocational programmes and others in regard to interests in and desires for a good education and the value of academic/theoretical knowledge. This is in line with lower secondary school research showing students generally to be highly concerned about the quality of their teaching and that they act to improve it (Öhrn, 2004).

Finally, if there is a dividing line with respect to subjectively expressed interests in a theoretical or practical education, it is between programmes that have clear orientation/identity and focus on the future with respect to positions or specific occupations and those that do not. In the material we examined, it is manifested in differences between on the one hand the Natural Science and Vehicle Programmes, and on the other the Child and Recreation and Individual Programmes. As argued, the Vehicle Programme differs from the other non-academic programmes in having a clear identity targeting a distinct occupation or set of occupations.

It might be argued that this clarity also makes it easier for students to identify and request from the school competencies needed for their future vocational life and career. We note, for instance, that Vehicle Programme students were strongly critical of the mathematics teaching they received because it was not sufficiently demanding. Like the Natural Science students, they requested maths instruction that was accurate and provided them with the means to cope with assumed future assignments and challenges. Similar demands and actions from students related to their future careers were not seen in the classes of programmes with weaker identities and labour market connections—the Social Science, Child and Recreation and Individual programmes.

Final comments

One of the overriding research questions addressed in our project, and to a large extent in the previous chapters, concerned the values and understandings of citizenship and democracy expressed in the education processes. It is apparent that the schools and teachers favoured students' individual voices and choices at the expense of collective student influence in all the studied cases. Thus, the students had a certain freedom of action when it came to sequencing their reading, the timing of tests and choice of text material in individual work, which can be seen as a way of fostering the self-governing, performance-oriented persons that post-industrial Sweden is commonly supposed to require (cf. Österlind, 1998; Lindblad, Lundahl, Lindgren and Zackari, 2002; Dovemark, 2004a).

Such an understanding of citizenship and democracy may partly explain the relative scarcity of collective actions and their lack of success. However, surveys indicate that students are in favour of collective action in order to acquire influence (cf. chapter two), that is the individualistic discourse does not seem to be deeply rooted among young Swedes, at least not in this sense. As we have seen in the previous chapters, joint initiatives from the students to influence the core of teaching—that is its level, contents and methods—seem to receive especially little encouragement.

Such actions constitute a threat to strong classification and framing of upper secondary education. Hence, the defence of teachers' knowledge-based superiority, particularly in subjects within a vertical discourse, still constitutes the greatest obstacle for students' initiation and carrying through of actions aiming to change aspects of education and for other adults in school to interfere and support such efforts of change.

References

Alderson, P., (2000) School students' views on school councils and daily life at school, *Children and Society,* 14(2): 121–134.

Almgren, E., (2006) *Att fostra demokrater. Om skolan i demokratin och demokratin i skolan,* [Fostering democrates. The school in democracy and democracy in school, in Swedish], Thesis (Phd), Uppsala University.

Angus, L., (2009) Problematizing neighbourhood renewal: Community, school effectiveness and disadvantage, *Critical Studies in Education,* 50(1), 37–50.

Apple, M. W. and Beane J. A., (2007) Lessons from democratic schools, in Apple M.W. and J. A. Beane (eds.), *Democratic schools. Lessons in powerful education*, Portsmouth: Heinemann.

Archer, L. and Francis, B., (2005) Constructions of racism by British Chinese pupils and parents, *Race, Ethnicity and Education*, 8(4), 387–407.

Archer, L., Pratt, S. D. and Phillips, D., (2001) Working-class men's constructions of masculinity and negotiations of (non) participation in higher education, *Gender and Education,* 13(4): 431–449.

Arnesen, A.-L., Lahelma, E. and Öhrn, E., (2008) Travelling discourses on gender and education: The case of boys' underachievement, *Nordisk pedagogik,* 28(1): 1–14.

Arnesen, A.-L. and Lundahl, L., (2006) Still social and democratic? Inclusive education policies in the Nordic welfare states, *Scandinavian Journal of Educational Research,* 50(3): 285–300.

Arnman, G. and Järnek, M., (2006) Ett könsperspektiv på tjugo års förändringar i gymnasieskolan och på arbetsmarknaden [A gender perspective on 20 years of change in upper secondary education and at the labor market, in Swedish], in *Könsskillnader i måluppfyllelse och utbildningsval,* Rapporter 287, Stockholm: Skolverket.

Arnot, M., (2002) *Reproducing Gender? Essays on educational theory and feminist politics,* London: RoutledgeFalmer.

Arnot, M., (2004) Male working class identities and social justice: a reconsideration of Paul Willis's Learning to labor in light of contemporary research, in Dolby, N., Dimitriadis, G. and Willis, P. E., (eds.), *Learning to labor in new times.* New York: RoutledgeFalmer.

Arnot, M., (2006) Freedom's children: a gender perspective on the education of the learner citizen, *International Review of Education, 52*(1): 67–87.

Arnot, M., David, M. and Weiner, G., (1999) *Closing the gender gap. Postwar education and social change,* Cambridge: Polity Press.

Arnot, M. and Dillabough, J.-A., (2000) *Challenging democracy: International perspectives on gender, education and citizenship,* London: RoutledgeFalmer.

Arnot , M. and Reay, D., (2004) The framing of pedagogic encounters: Regulating the social order in classroom learning, in Muller, J., Davies, B. and Morais, A., (eds.) *Reading Bernstein, researching Bernstein,* London: RoutledgeFalmer.

Arnot, M. and Reay, D., (2007) A sociology of pedagogic voice: power, inequality and pupil consultation, *Discourse: Studies in the Cultural Politics of Education,* 28(3): 311–325.

Ball, D. L., Goffney, I. M. and Bass, H., (2005) The role of mathematics instruction in building a socially just and diverse democracy, *The Mathematics Educator*, 15(1): 2–6.

Ball, S. J., (1981) *Beachside comprehensive: A case study of comprehensive schooling*, Cambridge: Cambridge University Press.

Ball, S. J., (2003) The teachers' soul and the terrors of performativity, *Journal of Education Policy*, 18(2), 215–228.

Beach, D., (1995) *Making sense of the problems of change: an ethnographic study of a teacher education reform*, Thesis (Phd), University of Gothenburg.

Beach, D., (1999a) Matematikutbildningens politik och ideologi [The policy and ideology of mathematics, in Swedish], *Nämnaren*, 26(3): 56–61.

Beach, D., (1999b) Om demokrati, reproduktion och förnyelse i dagens gymnasieskola, [Democracy, reproduction and renewal in upper-secondary school, in Swedish], *Pedagogisk forskning i Sverige*, 4(4): 349–365.

Beach, D., (1999c) D4.1.1 *Ethics, privacy and community implications—first version*. Project workpackage deliverable. Bryssel: EU arkiv ESPRIT

Beach, D., (2000) Continuing Problems of Teacher Education Reform, *Scandinavian Journal of Educational Research*, 44(3): 275–291.

Beach, D., (2003) Mathematics goes to market, in Beach, D., Gordon, T. and Lahelma, E., (eds.), *Democratic education: Ethnographic Challenges*, London: the Tufnell Press.

Beach, D., (2005) The problem of how learning should be socially organised, relations between reflection and transformative action, *Reflective Practice: International and Multidisciplinary Perspectives*, 6(4): 473–489.

Beach, D., (2008a) Ethnography and representation: about representations for criticism and change through ethnography, in Walford, G., (ed.) *How to do educational ethnography*, London: the Tufnell Press.

Beach, D., (2008b) The paradoxes of student learning preferences, *Ethnography and Education*, 3(2): 145–159.

Beach, D., (2008c) The changing relations between education professionals, the state and citizen consumers in Europe: Rethinking restructuring as capitalisation, *European Educational Research Journal*, 7(2): 195–207.

Beach, D., (2010) Identifying and comparing Scandinavian ethnography: comparisons and influences, *Ethnography and Education*, 5(1): 49–63.

Beach, D. and Bagley, C. A., (2010) New threats in advanced knowledge-based economies to the old problem of developing and sustaining quality teacher education, *The 2010 Teacher education policy in Europe conference, Sept 30th—Oct 2nd*, Tallinn, Estonia.

Beach, D. and Dovemark, M., (2007) *Education and the commodity problem: Ethnographic investigations of creativity and performativity in Swedish schools*, London: the Tufnell Press.

Beach, D. and Dovemark, M., (2009) Making right choices: An ethnographic investigation of creativity and performativity in four Swedish schools, *Oxford Review of Education*, 35(6): 689–704.

Berggren, I., (2001) *Identitet, kön och klass: Hur arbetarflickor formar sin identitet* [Identity, gender and class: How working class girls shape their identity, in Swedish], Thesis (Phd), University of Gothenburg.

Berglund, I., (2009) *Byggarbetsplatsen som skola—eller skolan som byggarbetsplats?: En studie av byggnadsarbetares yrkesutbildning*, [Construction site as school—or school as construction site? A study of vocational education and training for workers within building and construction, in Swedish], Thesis (Phd), Stockholm University.

Bergström, G., (1993) *Jämlikhet och kunskap: debatter och reformstrategier i socialdemokratisk skolpolitik 1975–1990* [Equality and knowledge: debates and reform strategies in social democratic education politics 1975–1990, in Swedish], Thesis (Phd), Stockholm University.

Bernstein, B., (1971) *Class, codes and control. Vol. 1: Theoretical studies towards a sociology of language*, London: Routledge.

Bernstein, B., (1975) *Class, codes and control. Vol. 3: Towards a theory of education transmissions*, London: Open University Press.

Bernstein, B., (1990) *Class, codes and control. Vol. 4: The structuring of pedagogic discourse*, London: Routledge.

Bernstein, B., (2000) *Pedagogy, symbolic control and identity: Theory, research, critique*, rev. ed., Lanham, Maryland: Rowman & Littlefield.

Bernstein, B., (2003) Social Class and Pedagogical Practice. In Bernstein, B., (ed.), *Class, codes and control. Vol 4: The structuring of pedagogic discourse*. London: Routledge.

Bertilsson, E., (2007) *Lärarna på skolans kungsväg: Om det naturvetenskapliga programmet på några gymnasier i Uppsala* [The teachers at the school's royal road: the Natural Science Programme in upper secondary schools in Uppsala, in Swedish], Uppsala: SEC, ILU, Uppsala University.

Borgnakke, K., (2004) Ethnographic studies and analysis of a recurrent theme: Learning by doing, *European Educational Research Journal*, 3(3): 539–565.

Bourdieu, P., (1994) *Praktiskt förnuft: bidrag till en handlingsteori* [The logic of practice, in Swedish], Göteborg: Daidalos.

Broady, D. and Börjesson, M., (2006) En social karta över gymnasieskolan [A social map of the upper secondary school, in Swedish], *Ord & Bild*, 2006(3–4): 90–99.

Broady, D., Börjesson, M., Bertilsson, E., Larsson, E,, Lidegran I. and Nordqvist, I., (2009) Skolans kungsväg: Det naturvetenskapliga programmets plats i utbildningssystemet [The Royal Road of schooling: The science programme within the Swedish educational system, in Swedish], in *Resultatdialog 2009: aktuell forskning om lärande*, Stockholm: Vetenskapsrådet.

Broady, D. and Gustafsson, J-E., (eds.) (2000) *Välfärd och skola: antologi från Kommittén Välfärdsbokslut,* [Welfare and schooling, in Swedish], SOU 2000:39, Stockholm: Fritzes offentliga publikationer.

Bronäs, A., (2003) Demokratins ansikte [The face of democracy, in Swedish], in Jonsson, B. and Roth, K., (eds.), *Demokrati och lärande. Om valfrihet, gemenskap och övervägande i skola och samhälle*, Lund: Studentlitteratur.

Bunar, N., (2008) The free schools 'riddle': between traditional social democratic, neo-liberal and multicultural tenets, *Scandinavian Journal of Educational Research*, 52(4): 423–438.

Burgess, R. G., (1995) *In the field: An introduction to field research*, 2 ed., London: Routledge.

Båth, S., (2006) *Kvalifikation och medborgarfostran: en analys av reformtexter avseende gymnasieskolans samhällsuppdrag,* [Qualification and citizenship education: a study of reform texts with reference to the social mission of the upper secondary school, in Swedish], Thesis (Phd), University of Gothenburg.

Carrington, B., Francis, B., Hutchings, M., Skelton, C., Read, B. and Hall, I., (2007) Does the gender of the teacher really matter? Seven- to eight-year-olds' accounts of their interactions with their teachers. *Educational Studies*, 33(4): 397–413.

Christiansen, I. M., (2008) Some tensions in mathematics education for democracy, in Sriraman, B., (ed.), *International perspectives on social justice in mathematics education*, pp. 69-86, Missoula: The University of Montana.

Colnerud, G., (1995) *Etik och praktik i läraryrket: en empirisk studie av lärares yrkesetiska konflikter i grundskolan*, [Ethics and practice in teaching: an empirical study of teachers' ethical conflicts in comprehensive school, in Swedish], Thesis (Phd), Linköping University.

Connell, R. W., (1987) *Gender and power*, Cambridge: Polity Press.

Connell, R. W., (2002) *Gender*, Cambridge: Polity Press.

Connell, R. W. and Messerschmidt, J.W., (2005) Hegemonic masculinity: Rethinking the concept, *Gender & Society*, 19(6), 829–859.

Danell, M., Klerfelt, A., Runevad, K. and Trodden, K., (1999) *Inflytandets villkor: en rapport om 41 skolors arbete med elevinflytande*, [The conditions of influence, in Swedish], Stockholm: Statens skolverk.

Davies, L., (1994) Can students make a difference? International perspectives on transformative education, *International Studies in Sociology of Education*, 4(1): 43–56.

Davies, L., (1999) Comparing definitions of democracy in education, *Compare: a Journal of Comparative and International Education*, 29(2): 127–140.

Davies, L., (2002) Pupil voice in Europe, in Schweisfurth, M., Davies, L. and Harber, C., (eds.), *Learning democracy and citizenship: international experiences*, Oxford: Symposium Books.

Davies, L., (2004) *Education and conflict: complexity and conflict*, London: Routledge.

Demokratiutredningen, (2000) *En uthållig demokrati!: politik för folkstyrelse på 2000-talet: Demokratiutredningens betänkande*, [A sustainable democracy! in Swedish], SOU 2000:1, Stockholm: Fritzes offentliga publikationer.

Denvall, V., (1999) Elevinflytandets realiteter [The realities of students' influence, in Swedish], in Amnå, E., (ed.) *Det unga folkstyret*, SOU 1999:93, Stockholm: Fakta info direkt.

Dolby, G, Dimitradis, G. and Willis, P., (2004) (eds.), *Learning to labor in new times*, New York: RoutledgeFalmer.

Dovemark, M., (2004a) *Ansvar—flexibilitet—valfrihet: En etnografisk studie om en skola i förändring*, [Responsibility—flexibility—freedom of choice: An ethnographic study of a school in transition, in Swedish], Thesis (Phd), University of Gothenburg.

Dovemark, M., (2004b) Pupil responsibility in the context of school changes in Sweden: market constraints on state policies for a creative education, *European Educational Research Journal*, 3(3), 657–672.

Dovemark, M., (2007) *Ansvar—Hur lätt är det? Om en skola i förändring*, [Responsibility—How easy is that? About a school in transmission, in Swedish], Lund: Studentlitteratur.

Dovemark, M., (2008) *En skola—skilda världar. Segregering på valfrihetens grund—om kreativitet och performativitet i den svenska grundskolan*. [One school—different worlds. Segregation on the basis of choice—about creativity and performativity within the Swedish compulsory school, in Swedish], Borås: Department of Education, Borås University.

Dovemark, M., (2010) Teachers' collective actions, alliances and resistance within neo-liberal ideas of education: the example of the individual programme, *European Education Research Journal*, 9(2), 232–244.

Dresch, J. and Lovén, A., (2010) Vägen efter grundskolan, in Lundahl, L., (ed.) *Bana vägen mot framtiden: Karriärval och vägledning i individuellt och politiskt perspektiv*, [Paving the road to the future: Career choice and career counseling in individual and political perspective, in Swedish], Lund: Studentlitteratur.

Edlund, U., (2010) Uppdrag: Rädda jobben, [Mission: Save the jobs, in Swedish], *Lärarnas tidning*, February 2.

Ekman, T., (2007) *Demokratisk kompetens: om gymnasiet som demokratiskola*, [Democratic competence: democratic learning in gymnasium/upper secondary school, in Swedish], Thesis (Phd), University of Gothenburg.

Englund, T., (1999) Den svenska skolan och demokratin: Möjligheter och begränsningar [The Swedish schooling and democracy: Opportunities and limitations, in Swedish], in Amnå, E., (ed.) *Det unga folkstyret*, SOU 199:93, Stockholm: Fakta info direkt.

Englund, T., (2000) *Deliberativa samtal som värdegrund—historiska perspektiv och aktuella förutsättningar*, [Deliberative communication as fundamental values—historical perspectives and contemporary conditions, in Swedish], Stockholm: Skolverket.

Englund, T., (2003) Skolan och demokratin—på väg mot en skola för deliberativa samtal? [School and democracy—towards a school for deliberative communication, in Swedish], in Jonsson, B. and Roth, K., (eds.), *Demokrati och lärande: Om valfrihet, gemenskap och övervägande i skola och samhälle*, Lund: Studentlitteratur.

Englund, T., (2004) *Utbildningpolitiskt systemskifte?* [Educational policy change?, in Swedish], Stockholm: HSL Förlag.

Epstein, D., (1998) Real boys don't work: 'underachievement', masculinity and the harassment of 'sissies', in Epstein, D., Elwood, J., Hey, V. and Man, J., (eds.), *Failing boys? Issues in gender and achievement*, Buckingham: Open University Press.

Eriksson, L., (red.) (2009) *Universitet & högskolor: Högskoleverkets årsrapport. 2009*, [Universities & colleges: Swedish Agency for Higher Education's Annual Report. 2009, in Swedish], Stockholm: Högskoleverket.

Erixon Arreman, I. and Holm, A.-S., (2011) Privatisation of public education? The emergence of independent upper secondary schools in Sweden, *Journal of Education Policy*, 26(2): 225-243.

Erixon Arreman, I., Lundahl, L. and Schedin, G., (2009) Marketing and competition—part of everyday life and pedagogic identities in upper secondary school? *The annual ECER Conference, 28–30 September*, Vienna.

Falk, E.-M., (1999) *Lärare tar gestalt: En hermeneutisk studie av texter om lärarblivande på distans*, [Teachers take shape: a hermeneutical study of texts on becoming a teacher through distance education, in Swedish], Thesis (Phd), Uppsala University.

Forsberg, E., (2000) *Elevinflytandets många ansikten*, [The many faces of school student impact, in Swedish], Thesis (Phd), Uppsala university.

Francis, B., (1999) Lads, lasses and (new) labour: 14—16 year-old students' responses to the 'laddish behaviour and boys' underachievement debate', *British Journal of Sociology of Education*, 20(3): 355–371.

Francis, B. and Skelton, C., (2001) Men teachers and the construction of heterosexual masculinity in the classroom, *Sex Education*, 1(1): 9–21.

Francis, B., Skelton, C. and Read, B., (2010) The simultaneous production of educational achievement and popularity: How do some pupils accomplish it?, *British Educational Research Journal*, 36(2): 317–340.

Frosh, S., Phoenix, A. and Pattman, R., (2002) *Young masculinities: Understanding boys in contemporary society*, Basingstoke: Palgrave.

Gamble, J., (2006) Theory and practice in the vocational curriculum, in Young, M. and Gamble, J., (eds.) *Knowledge, curriculum and qualifications for South African further education*, Cape Town: HSRC Press.

Giddens, A., (1984a) *The constitution of society*, Cambridge: Polity Press.

Giddens, A., (1984b) *The constitution of society*, Berkeley: University of California Press.

Gordon, T., (2006) Girls in education: citizenship, agency and emotions, *Gender and Education*, 18(1): 1–15.

Gordon, T. and Holland, J., (2003) Nation space: the construction of citizenship and difference in schools, in Beach, D., Gordon, T. and Lahelma, E., (eds.), *Democratic education: ethnographic challenges*, London: the Tufnell Press.

Gordon, T., Holland, J. and Lahelma, E., (2000) *Making spaces: Citizenship and difference in schools*, Basingstoke: Macmillan Press.

Gordon, T., Holland, J. and Lahelma, E., (2000) Friends or foes? Interpreting relations between girls in school, in Walford, G. and Hudson, C., (eds.), *Genders and Sexualities in Educational Ethnography*, Greenwich, Connecticut: JAI.

Gordon, T., Holland, J., Lahelma, E. and Thomson R., (2008) Young female citizens in education: emotions, resources and agency, *Pedagogy, Culture & Society*, 16(2): 177–191.

Gordon, T., Hynninen, P., Lahelma, E., Metso, T., Palmu, T. and Tolonen, T., (2006) Collective ethnography, joint experiences and individual pathways, *Nordisk Pedagogik*, 26(1): 3–15.

Gordon, T., Lahelma, E. and Beach, D., (2003) Introduction Marketisation of democratic education: Ethnographic insights, in Beach, D., Gordon, T. and Lahelma, E., (eds.), *Democratic education: Ethnographic challenges*, London: the Tufnell Press.

Govt. Bill 1968:140 *Angående riktlinjer för det frivilliga skolväsendet* [Regarding guidelines for non-compulsory education, in Swedish], Stockholm: Ministry of Education.

Govt. Bill 1990/91:85. *Växa med kunskaper — om gymnasieskolan och vuxenutbildningen* [Growing With and By Knowledge — on Upper Secondary and Adult Education, in Swedish], Stockholm: Ministry of Education.

Hamilton, D., (1989) *Towards a theory of schooling*, London: Falmer Press.

Hammersley, M. and Atkinson, P., (1995) *Ethnography: Principles in practice*, London: Routledge.

Hammersley, M. and Atkinson, P., (2007) *Ethnography: Principles in Practice, 3 ed.*, London: Routledge.

Hansson, M. E., (2009) Tre av fyra kommuner skär ner i skolan, [Three of four municipalities make cutbacks in school, in Swedish], *Svenska Dagbladet*, 6 May.

Hansson, K. and Lundahl, L., (2004) Youth politics and local constructions of youth, *British Journal of Sociology of Education*, 25(2): 161–178.

Hedencrona, E. and Smed-Gerdin, K., (2007) *Blickpunkt — fordon*, [Centre-stage — vehicles, in Swedish], Malmö: Gleerups.

Henderson, S. and Hudson, B., (2010) What is subject content knowledge in mathematics?, *The 2010 Teacher Education Policy in Europe Conference, Sept 30th — Oct 2nd*, Tallinn, Estonia.

Henriksson, C., (2004) *Living away from blessings: school failure as lived experience,* Thesis (Phd), Växjö University.

Hjelmér, C., Lappalainen, S. and Rosvall, P.-Å., (2010) Time, space and young people's agency in vocational upper secondary education: A cross cultural perspective, *European Educational Research Journal,* 9(2): 245–256.

Holm, A.-S., (2008) *Relationer i skolan—en studie av femininiteter och maskuliniteter i år 9,* [Relations in school: A study of feminities and masculinities in the 9th grade, in Swedish], Thesis (Phd), University of Gothenburg.

Holm, A.-S. and Öhrn, E., (2007) Crossing boundaries? Complexities and drawbacks to gendered success stories, in Carlson, M., Rabo, A., Gök, F., (eds.) *Education in 'multicultural' societies: Turkish and Swedish perspectives,* Istanbul: Tauris.

Hoskins, B., d'Hombres, B. and Campbell, J., (2008) *European Educational Research Journal,* 7(3): 386–402.

Hugo, M., (2007) *Liv och lärande i gymnasieskolan. En studie om elevers och lärares erfarenheter av en liten grupp på gymnasieskolans individuella program,* [Life and learning in upper secondary school. A study of students' and teachers' experiences of a small group at the individual programme in upper secondary school, in Swedish], Thesis (Phd), Jönköping University.

Hultin, E., (2008) Gymnasiereformen och svenskämnets traditioner, [The Swedish upper secondary school reform and the teaching traditions of the subject Swedish, in Swedish], *Utbildning och Demokrati,* 17(1): 99–108.

Hultqvist, E., (2001) *Segregerande integrering: En studie av gymnasieskolans individuella program,* [Segregating integrating: A study about the individual programme at upper secondary school, in Swedish], Thesis (Phd), Stockholm University.

Jackson, C., (2002) Laddishness as a self-worth protection strategy, *Gender and Education,* 14(1): 37–50.

Jackson, C., (2006) *Lads and ladettes in school: Gender and a fear of failure,* Maidenhead: Open University Press.

Jeffrey, B. and Troman, G., (2004) Time for Etnography, *British Educational Research Journal,* 30(4), 535–548.

Jeffrey, B. and Woods, P., (1998) *Testing teachers: the effect of school inspections on primary teachers,* London: Falmer Press.

Jenkins, S. P., Micklewright, J. and Schnepf, S. V., (2006) Social segregation in secondary schools: How does England compare with other countries? *ISER Working Paper* 2006-2, Coldchester: Institute for Social & Economic Research, University of Essex, www.iser.essex.ac.uk/publications/working-papers/iser/2006-02.pdf [Accessed 25 August 2010].

Johansson, M., (2009) *Anpassning och motstånd: En etnografisk studie av gymnasieelevers institutionella identitetsskapande* [Adaption and resistance: An ethnographic investigation of the development of institutional identities amongst upper secondary school pupils, in Swedish], Thesis (Phd), University of Gothenburg.

Johansson, S., (2007) *Dom under trettio, vem bryr sig och varför? Ungdomars värdering och politiska deltagande,*[Those under thirty, who cares and why? Young people's values and political participation, in Swedish], Thesis (Phd), University of Gothenburg.

Jönsson, I., (2006) Utbildningsskillnader—stabilitet och förändring i ett europeiskt perspektiv [Educational differences—stability and change in a European perspective, in Swedish], in *Könsskillnader i måluppfyllelse och utbildningsval,* Stockholm: Skolverket.

Kamperin, R.-M., (2005a) *Försök att påverka: delrapport 1: en empirisk studie av ungdomars vilja och möjlighet att förändra: analys av tre påverkanssituationer i skolmiljön* [Attempts to influence: report 1: an empirical study of young people's intentions and possibilities to make changes: analysis of three influencing situations in school environment, in Swedish], Department of Education: University of Gothenburg.

Kamperin, R.-M., (2005b) *Försök att påverka: delrapport 2: en empirisk studie av ungdomarnas påverkansmöjligheter i tre grundskoleklasser* [Attempts to influence: report 2: an empirical study of young people's possibilities to influence in three compulsory school classes, in Swedish], Department of Education: University of Gothenburg.

Karlsson, A.-M., (2009) Positioned by reading and writing: literacy practices, roles and genres in common occupations, *Written Communication*, 26(1): 53–76.

Keddie, N., (1971) Classroom knowledge, in Young, M., (ed.) *Knowledge and control: new directions for the sociology of education*, London: Macmillan.

Kommittén Välfärdsbokslut, (2000) *Välfärd och skola: antologi från Kommittén Välfärdsbokslut*, [Welfare and schooling, in Swedish], SOU 2000:39, Stockholm: Fritzes offentliga publikationer.

Korp, H., (2006) *Lika chanser på gymnasiet? En studie om betyg, nationella prov och social reproduktion*, [Equal chances in upper secondary education? A study on grades, national assessments and social reproduction, in Swedish], Thesis (Phd), Malmö University.

Krantz, J., (2005) *Om bedömning av demokratisk kompetens: Kontextuella och principiella aspekter* [On assessing democratic competence: Contextual and principle aspects], Växjö: Department of Education, Växjö University.

Kryger, N., (1990) Drengepædagogik? [Pedagogics for boys?, in Danish], in Jacobsen, H. and Højgaard, L., (eds.), *Skolen er køn*, Copenhagen: Ligestillingsrådet.

Lahelma, E., (2000) Lack of male teachers: A problem for students or teachers? *Pedagogy, Culture and Society*, 8(2): 173–186.

Lahelma, E. and Öhrn, E., (2003) Strong Nordic women in the making? Gender policies and classroom practices, in Beach, D., Gordon, T. and Lahelma, E., (eds.), *Democratic education: ethnographic challenges*, London: the Tufnell Press.

Larsson, S., (2006) Ethnography in action. How ethnography was established in Swedish educational research, *Ethnography and Education*, 1(2): 177–195.

Lemar, S., (2001) *Kaoskompetens och gummibandspedagogik: en studie av karaktärsäm- neslärare i en decentraliserad gymnasieorganisation* [Chaos competence and rubber- band-pedagogy: a study of Programme-related subject teachers in a decentralised upper secondary school organisation, in Swedish], Thesis (Phd), Umeå University.

Lidegran, I., (2009) *Utbildningskapital: Om hur det alstras, fördelas och förmedlas*, [Educational capital: Its creation, distribution and transmission, in Swedish], Thesis (Phd), Uppsala university.

Lidegran, I., Börjesson, M., Nordqvist I. and Broady, D., (2006) I korsningen mellan kön och klass: Gymnasieskolan i riket, i Uppsala och i Gävle [At the intersection between gender and class: Upper secondary education in Sweden, in Uppsala and in Gävle, in Swedish], in *Könsskillnader i måluppfyllelse och utbildningsval*, Stockholm: Skolverket.

Liljestrand, J., (2002) *Klassrummet som diskussionsarena*, [The classroom as an arena for discussions, in Swedish], Thesis (Phd), Örebro University.

Lindberg, V., (2003a) Learning practices in vocational education, *Scandinavian Journal of Educational Research,* 47(2): 157–179.

Lindberg, V., (2003b) Vocational knowing and the content in vocational education, *Scandinavian Journal of Educational research,* 47(2): 157–179.

Lindberg, V., (2003c) *Yrkesutbildning i omvandling: En studie av lärarpraktiker och kunsk apstransformationer,* [Vocational Education in Change: A study of learning practices and knowledge transformations, in Swedish], Stockholm: HLS Förlag.

Lindblad, S., Lundahl, L., Lindgren, J. and Zackari, G., (2002) Educating for the New Sweden. *Scandinavian Journal of Educational Research,* 46(3), 283–303.

Lund, S., (2008) Choice paths in the Swedish upper secondary education—A critical discourse analysis of recent reforms, *Journal of Education Policy,* 23(6): 633–648.

Lundahl, L., (1997) A Common Denominator? Swedish employers, trade unions and vocational education, *International Journal of Training and Development,* 1(2): 91–103.

Lundahl, L., (1998) Still the Stepchild of Swedish Educational Politics? Vocational Education and Training in Sweden in the 1990s, *TNTEE Publications,* 1(1): 39–53.

Lundahl, L., (2002) Sweden: Decentralization, deregulation, quasi-markets—and then what? *Journal of Education Policy,* 17(6): 687–697.

Lundahl, L., (2008) Skilda framtidsvägar—perspektiv på det tidiga 2000-talets gymnasiereform, [Separate paths to the future: Perspectives on the Swedish upper seconddary school reform of the early 2000s, in Swedish], *Utbildning och Demokrati,* 17(1): 29–51.

Lundahl, L., Erixon Arreman, I., Lundström, U. and Rönnberg, L., (2010) Setting things right?: Swedish upper secondary school reform in a 40-year perspective, *European Journal of Education,* 45(1): 46–59.

Lundgren, A.-S., (2000) *Tre år i g: perspektiv på kropp och kön i skolan,* [Three years in g: perspectives on body and gender in school, in Swedish], Eslöv: Symposion.

Lundin, S., (2008) *Skolans matematik: en kritisk analys av den svenska skolmatematikens förhistoria, uppkomst och utveckling* [The mathematics of schooling: a critical analysis of the prehistory, birth and development of Swedish mathematics education; in Swedish], Thesis (Phd), Uppsala University.

Lundström, M., (1999) Demokrati i skolan? [Democracy in school? (in Swedish)] in Amnå, E., (ed.) *Det unga folkstyret,* SOU 1999:93, Stockholm: Fakta info direkt.

Lynch, K. and Lodge, A., (2002) *Equality and power in schools: Redistribution, recognition and representation,* Abingdon: RoutledgeFalmer.

Mac an Ghaill, M., (1994) *The making of men: Masculinities, sexualities and schooling,* Buckingham: Open University press.

Mikkelsen, R., (2003) All-European study on policies for education and democratic citizenship (EDC). The Northern Europe region. E.D.C. Documents and publications,www.coe.int/T/e/Cultural_Cooperation/Education/E.D.C/Documents_ and_publications/ [Accessed 30 September 2010].

Ministry of Education (1992) SFS 1992:394 *Gymnasieförordningen* [Ordinance of Upper secondary Education]. www.skolverket.se/sb/d/2218/a/12461 [Accessed 4 July 2010].

Ministry of Education and Ecclesiastical Affairs, (1948) *1946 års skolkommissions betänkande med förslag till riktlinjer för det svenska skolväsendets utveckling* [The 1946 Parliamentary Committee report with proposed guidelines for developing the school system, in Swedish], SOU 1948:27, Stockholm: Ecklesistatikdepartementet.

Ministry of Education and Research, (1994) *Läroplaner för de frivilliga skolformerna: Lpf 94* [Curriculum for the non-compulsory school system: Lpf 94, in Swedish], Stockholm: Fritzes.

Ministry of Education and Research, (2008) *Framtidsvägen—en reformerad gymnasieskola. Betänkande*, [The future road—Reformed upper secondary education. Report, in Swedish], SOU 2008:27, Stockholm: Fritzes.

Ministry of Education and Research (2010) SFS 2010:235 Förordning om ändring i gymnasieförordningen (1992:394) [Ordinance on amendment of the ordinance of upper secondary education 1992:394, in Swedish], Stockholm: Utbildningsdepartementet. www.lagboken.se/dokument/Andrings-SFS/620349/SFS-2010_235-Forordning-om-andring-i-gymnasieforordningen-1992_394?id=50519 [Accessed 4 July 2010].

Namukasa, I., (2004) School mathematics in the era of globalization, *Interchange: a Quarterly Review of Education*, 35(2), 209–227.

Nilsson, N.-E., (2002) *Skriv med egna ord: En studie av läroprocesser när elever i grundskolans senare år skriver 'forskningsrapporter'*,[Write with your own words: A study of learning processes when pupils in secondary school write 'research reports', in Swedish], Thesis, (Phd), Malmö University.

Nixon, D., (2009) 'I can't put a smiley face on': Working-class masculinity, emotional labour and service work in the 'new economy', *Gender, Work and Organization*, 16(3): 300–322.

Norlund, A., (2009) *Kritisk sakprosaläsning i gymnasieskolan: Didaktiska perspektiv på läroböcker, lärare och nationella prov*, [Critical reading of non-fiction in upper secondary school: Didactical perspectives on textbooks, teachers and national tests, in Swedish], Thesis (Phd), University of Gothenburg.

Nylund, M., (2010) Framtidsvägen: Vägen till vilken framtid för eleverna på gymnasieskolans yrkesprogram? [The road to the future: The road to what future for the students on vocational programmes at upper secondary school?, in Swedish] *Pedagogisk Forskning i Sverige*, 15(1): 33–52.

Nyroos, M., Rönnberg, L. and Lundahl, L., (2004) A matter of timing: time use, freedom and influence in school from a pupil perspective, *European Educational Research Journal*, 3(4): 743–758.

OECD, (2005) *European year of citizenship through education: Learning and living democracy*, Strasbourg.

Ohlsson, M., (1995) Samtal i skolan. Om språk och kön, [Conversations in school: Language and gender, in Swedish], *Utbildning och Demokrati*, 4(3): 44–64.

Öhrn, E., (1990) *Könsmönster i klassrumsinteraktion.En observations- och intervjustudie av högstadieelevers lärarkontakter* [Gender patterns in classroom interactions. Observations and interviews concerning students' interactions with teachers in grade nine of the comprehensive school], Thesis [PhD], University of Gothenburg.

Öhrn, E., (1998) Gender and power in school: On girls' open resistance, *Social Psychology of Education, 1(4)*: 341–357.

Öhrn, E., (2000) Changing patterns? Reflections on contemporary Swedish research on gender and education, *Nordic Journal of Women's Studies*, 8(3): 128–136.

Öhrn, E., (2001) Marginalization of democratic values: a gendered practice of schooling?, *International Journal of Inclusive Education*, 5(2/3): 319–328.

Öhrn, E., (2002a) *Könsmönster i förändring? En kunskapsöversikt om unga i skolan*, [Gender-patterns changing? A review of research on young people in education, in Swedish], Stockholm: Skolverket.

Öhrn, E., (2002b) Jämställdhet som en del av skolans värdegrund: Om kön, klass och etnicitet i skolvardagen, [Gender equality as part of the school's fundamental values. On gender, class and ethnicity in everyday schooling, in Swedish], in Frånberg, G.-M. and Kallós, D., (eds.), *Demokrati i skolans vardag. Fem nordiska forskare rapporterar*, Umeå Universitet.

Öhrn, E., (2004) Young people as political actors in school, *The European Conference for Educational Research, 22–25, September,* University of Crete, Greece.

Öhrn, E., (2005) *Att göra skillnad. En studie av ungdomar som politiska aktörer i skolans vardag,* [To make a difference. A study of young people as political actors in schools, in Swedish], Göteborg: Department of Education, University of Gothenburg.

Öhrn, E., (2009) Challenging sexism? Gender and ethnicity in the secondary school, *Scandinavian Journal of Educational Research,* 53(6): 579–590.

Öhrn, E. and Weiner, G., (2009) The sound of silence! Reflections on inclusion and exclusion in the field of gender and education, *Gender and Education,* 21(4): 423–430.

Olofsson, J., Panican, A., Pettersson, L. and Righard, E., (2009). Ungdomars övergång från skola till arbetsliv—aktuella utmaningar och lokala erfarenheter, [Young people's transitions from school to working life—current challenges and local experiences, in Swedish], *Meddelanden från Socialhögskolan* 2009:1, Lund: Socialhögskolan, Lund University.

Olofsson, J. and Wadensjö, E., (2007) Ungdomar, utbildning och arbetsmarknad i Norden—lika men ändå olika, [Youth, education and labour market in Scandinavia—similar yet different, in Swedish], Stockholm: Forskningsrådet för arbetsliv och socialvetenskap.

Osbeck, C., Holm, A.-S. and Wernersson, I., (2003) *Kränkningar i skolan. Förekomst, former och sammanhang,* [Violations in school. Presence, forms and context, in Swedish], Göteborg: Värdegrunden, University of Gothenburg.

Oscarsson, V., (2005) *Elevers demokratiska kompetens: Rapport från den nationella utvärderingen av grundskolan 2003 (NU03)—samhällsorienterande ämnen,* [Students' democratic competence, in Swedish], Göteborg: Department of Education, University of Gothenburg.

Österlind, E., (1998). *Disciplinering via frihet: Elevers planering av sitt eget arbete,* [Disciplining via Freedom: Independent work and student planning, in Swedish], Thesis (Phd), Uppsala University.

Paechter. C. F., (1998) *Educating the other: gender, power and schooling,* London: Falmer Press.

Pattman, R., Frosh, S. and Phoenix, A., (2005) Constructing and experiencing boyhoods in research in London, *Gender and Education,* 17(5): 555–561.

Pellegrino, J. W. and Goldman, S. R., (2008) Beyond rhetoric: Realities and complexities of integrating assessment into classroom teaching and learning, in Dwyer, C. A., (ed.), *The future of assessment: Shaping teaching and learning,* New York: Lawrence Erlbaum Associates.

Persson, B., (2005) *Elevers olikheter och specialpedagogisk kunskap* [Pupil differences and special education knowledge], Stockholm: Liber.

Phoenix, A., (2004) Neoliberalism and masculinity: Racialization and the contradictions of schooling, *Youth & Society,* 36(2): 227–246.

Reay, D. and Mirza, H. S., (1997) Uncovering genealogies of the margins: *British Journal of Sociology of Education,* 18(4): 477–499.

Rönnlund, M., (2010) Student participation in activities with influential outcomes: issues of gender, individuality and collective thinking in Swedish secondary schools, *European Educational Research Journal,* 9(2): 208–219.

Sandell, A., (2007) Utbildningssegregation och självsortering: Om gymnasieval, genus och lokala praktiker, [Segregation and self-sorting in education: On choice of upper secondary education, gender and local practices, in Swedish], Thesis (PhD), Malmö University.

Selander, S., (2003) Skolans blick—världen som text, [The Gaze of School—the World as Text, in Swedish], in Selander, S., (ed.) *Kobran, nallen och majjen: Tradition och förnyelse i svensk skola och skolforskning,* Stockholm: Myndigheten för skolutveckling.

Sernhede, O., (2007) Urbanization of injustice, immigrant youth and informal schooling, in Noblit, G. W. and Pink, W. T., (eds.), *International handbook of urban education,* Dordrecht: Springer.

Sjöberg, L., (2009) Skolan och den 'goda' utbildningen—för ett konkurrenskraftigt europa, [Schools and 'good' education—for a competitive Europe, in Swedish] *Utbildning och Demokrati,* 18(1): 33–58.

Skeggs, B., (1991) Challenging masculinity and using sexuality, *British Journal of Sociology of Education,* 12(2): 127–139.

Skeggs, B., (1997) *Formations of class and gender: becoming respectable,* London: Sage.

Skovsmose, O., (1998) Linking mathematics education and democracy: Citizenship, mathematical archaeology and deliberative interaction, *ZDM—International Journal of Mathematics Education,* 30(6): 195–203.

Smith, J., (2007) 'Ye've got to 'ave balls to play this game sir!' Boys, peers and fears: the negative influence of school-based 'cultural accomplices' in constructing hegemonic masculinities, *Gender and Education,* 19(2): 179–198.

Sundberg, D., (2003) The politics of time in educational restructuring, in Beach, D., Gordon, T. and Lahelma, E., (eds.) *Democratic education: ethnographic challenges.* London: the Tufnell Press.

Svensson, A., (2001) Består den sociala snedrekryteringen? Elevens val av gymnasieprogram hösten 1998, [Does the uneven social recruitment remain? Students' choice of high school programme autumn 1998, in Swedish], *Pedagogisk Forskning i Sverige,* 6(3), 161–172.

Svensson, A., (2006) Hur skall rekryteringen till högskolans mest eftersökta utbildningar breddas?, [How to broaden recruitment to the most attractive programmes in higher education?, in Swedish], *Pedagogisk Forskning i Sverige,* 11(2), 116–133.

Svensson, A., (2007) Dagens gymnasieskola—bättre än sitt rykte?, [Present upper secondary education—better than its reputation?, in Swedish], *Pedagogisk Forskning i Sverige,* 12(4): 301–323.

Svingby, G., (1993) Manligt eller omoget? [Male or immature?, in Swedish] in *Visst är vi olika,* Stockholm: Utbildningsdepartementet.

Swedish National Agency for Education, (1999) *Läroplanerna i praktiken* [Curriculum in practice, in Swedish], Stockholm: Statens skolverk.

Swedish National Agency for Education, (2000) *Reformeringen av gymnasieskolan—en sammanfattande analys* [The Reformation of upper secondary school—a concluding analysis, in Swedish], Stockholm: Statens skolverk.

Swedish National Agency for Education (2001). *Programhäfte för IV*, [Programme booklet for the IV, in Swedish] Stockholm: Fritzes.

Swedish National Agency for Education, (2003) *Ung i demokratin: Gymnasieelevers kunskaper och attityder i demokrati- och samhällsfrågor*, [Young people in democracy: Knowledge and attitudes among upper secondary students, in Swedish], Stockholm: Skolverket, www.skolverket.se/publikationer?id=1180 [Accessed 16 December 2010].

Swedish National Agency for Education, (2004) *Elevmedverkan i skolans arbetsmiljöarbete genom elevskyddsombud* [Student participation in schools' work with their working environment by student safety representatives, in Swedish], Stockholm: Skolverket, www.skolverket.se/ publikationer?id=1201 [Accessed 16 December 2010].

Swedish National Agency for Education, (2007) *Heltid och resursförstärkning. Utvecklingen av individuella program*, [Full-time education and strengthening of resources. Development of individual programs, in Swedish], Stockholm: Skolverket, www.skolverket.se/publikationer?id=1715 [Accessed 5 August 2010].

Swedish National Agency for Education, (2009a) *Diskriminerad, trakasserad, kränkt?: Barns, elevers, studerandes uppfattningar om diskriminering och trakasserier*, [Discriminated, badgered, offended?: Children's, pupils' and students' apprehension about harassments and abusive treatment, in Swedish], Stockholm: Skolverket, www. skolverket.se/publikationer?id=2164 [Accessed 16 December 2010].

Swedish National Agency for Education, (2009b) *Vad påverkar resultaten i svensk grundskola? Kunskapsöversikt om betydelsen av olika faktorer*, [What influences the outcome of the Swedish elementary school? A review of the importance of various factors, in Swedish], Stockholm: Skolverket, www.skolverket.se/ publikationer?id=2260 [Accessed 16 December 2010].

Swedish National Agency for Education, (2009c) *Studieresultatet I gymnasieskolan—en statistisk beskrivning av ofullständiga gymnasiestudier*, [Study outcomes in upper secondary school—a statistical description of incomplete education at upper secondary level, in Swedish], Stockholm: Skolverket, www.skolverket.se/publikationer?id=1814 [Accessed 16 December 2010].

Swedish National Agency for Education, (2010a) *Morgondagens medborgare: ICCS 2009: svenska 14-åringars kunskaper, värderingar och deltagande i internationell belysning*, [Tomorrow's citizens. Swedish 14-year-olds knowledge, values and participation in an international perspective, in Swedish], Stockholm: Skolverket, www.skolverket.se/publikationer?id=2397 [Accessed 16 December 2010].

Swedish National Agency for Education, (2010b) *National level 2009: Swedens Official Statistics on pre-school activities, schoolage child care, schools and adult education. P. 2, Children, pupils and staff*, Stockholm: Skolverket, www.skolverket.se/ publikationer?id=2354 [Accessed 16 December 2010].

Swedish National Agency for Education, (2010c) *Konkurrensen om eleverna: kommunernas hantering av minskade gymnasiekullar och en växande skolmarknad*, [Competition over students: municipalities' management of decreased student cohorts in upper secondary school and a growing school market, in Swedish], Stockholm: Skolverket, www.skolverket.se/ publikationer?id=2394 [Accessed 16 December 2010].

Swedish National Agency for Education, (2010d) Skolor och elever i gymnasieskolan läsår 2008/09, [Schools and students in upper secondary education academic year 2008/09, in Swedish], Stockholm: Skolverket, www.skolverket.se/sb/d/1718/a/14862#paragraphAnchor2 [Accessed 1 October 2010].

Swedish National Agency for Education, (2010e) *Betyg i grundskolan läsår 2007/08, tabell 9A*, [Marks in compulsory school academic year 2007/08, table 9A, in Swedish], Stockholm: Skolverket, www.skolverket.se/ sb/d/1637/a/14358 [Accessed 10 October 2010].

Swedish National Agency for School Improvement, (2007) *Kvalitet inom IV—hela skolans ansvar* [Quality of the individual program—a responsibility of the whole school, in Swedish]. Stockholm: Myndigheten för Skolutveckling. www.skolverket. se/publikationer?id=1882 [Accessed 10 October 2010].

Swedish National Board of Education, (1970) *Läroplan för gymnasieskolan, Lgy 70* [Curriculum plan of upper secondary school, Lgy 70, in Swedish], Stockholm: Läromedelsförlaget.

Swedish National Board of Youth Affairs, (2001) *Ung i demokratin. Ungdomsstyrelsens sammanfattning av 14-15 åringars värderingar.* [Young in the democracy. The Swedish National Board of Youth's summary of 14-15 years olds' values, in Swedish]. Stockholm: Ungdomsstyrelsen.

Swedish Parliament, (2006) Svar på skriftlig fråga 2006/07, Elevmajoritetet i lokala skolstyrelser, Jan Björklund, den 22 november [Reply to written question 2006/07:143, Student majority in local school boards, Jan Björklund, 22 November, in Swedish] www.riksdagen.se/webbnav/ index.aspx?nid=71&dok_id=GU12143 [Accessed 10 October 2010].

Swedish Schools Inspectorate, (2010) *Skolornas arbete vid trakasserier och kränkande behandling,* [School Supervision quality review. The school's efforts at intimidation and abusive treatment, in Swedish], Rapport 2010:1, Stockholm: Skolinspektionen, www.skolinspektionen.se/ Documents/Kvalitetsgranskning/Trakasserier/slutrapport-trakasserier-ochkrankningar.pdf?epslanguage=sv [Accessed 20 December 2010].

Tallberg Broman, I., Rubinstein Reich, L., and Hägerström, J., (2002) *Likvärdighet i en skola för alla: Historisk bakgrund och kritisk granskning,* [From a class-, gender- and ethnicity-structured school to a school for everyone, in Swedish], Stockholm: Skolverket.

Thorne, B., (1993) *Gender play: Girls and boys in school,* New Brunswick, New Jersey: Rutgers University Press.

Trondman, M., (2008) Bypass surgery: Re-routing theory to ethnographic study, in Walford, G., (ed.), *How to do ethnography,* London: the Tufnell Press.

Turmo, A., (2004) Scientific literacy and socio-economic background among 15-year-olds: a Nordic perspective, *Scandinavian Journal of Educational Research,* 48(3): 287–305.

Walkerdine, V., (1990) *Schoolgirl fictions,* London: Verso.

Ve, H., (1982) Makt, intresse och socialisation, [Power, interest and socialisation, in Swedish], *Kvinnovetenskaplig tidskrift,* 3(2): 23–32.

Weis, L., (1990) *Working class without work: High school students in a de-industrializing economy.* New York: Routledge.

Wheelahan, L., (2007) How competency-based training locks the working class out of powerful knowledge: a modified Bernsteinian analysis, *British Journal of Sociology of Education,* 28(5): 637–651.

Willis, P., (1977) *Learning to labour,* Farnborough: Saxon House.

Willis, P., (2000) *The ethnographic imagination,* Cambridge: Polity Press.

Willis, P., (2004) 'Old Books, New Times', in Dolby, N. and Dimitradis, G., (eds.), *Learning to labor in new times*, London: Routledge.

Willis, P. and Trondman, M., (2000) Manifesto for ethnography, *Ethnography*, 1(1): 5–16.

Wilson, M., (Ed) (1991) *Girls and young women in education: A European perspective,* Oxford: Pergamon Press.

Vithal, R., (1999) Democracy and authority: A complementarity in mathematics education?, *ZDM – International Journal of Mathematics Education,* 31(1): 27–36.

Woods, P., (1979) *The divided school,* London: Routledge and Kegan Paul.

Young, M., (2006) Conceptualising vocational knowledge: Some theoretical considerations, in Young, M. and Gamble, J., (eds.) *Knowledge, Curriculum and Qualifications for South African Further Education,* Cape Town: HSRC Press.

Young, M., (2008) *Bringing knowledge back in: From social constructivism to social realism in sociology of education,* London: Routledge.

Yuval-Davis, N., (1997) *Gender and nation,* London: Sage.

www.ingramcontent.com/pod-product-compliance
Lightning Source LLC
Chambersburg PA
CBHW070920270326
41927CB00011B/2649